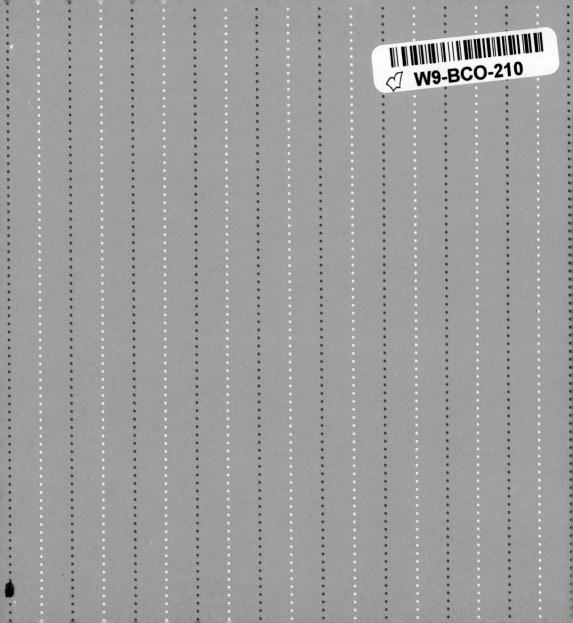

Simple Comforts

Simple Comforts

50 Heartwarming Recipes

Sur La Table

**Andrews McMeel
Publishing, LLC**

Kansas City • Sydney • London

10 11 12 13 14 WKT 10 9 8 7 6 5 4 3 2 1

ISBN: 978-0-7407-9351-6

Library of Congress Control Number: 2010924507

Recipes adapted from *Things Cooks Love, The Art and Soul of Baking, Knives Cooks Love, Tips Cooks Love,* and *Baking Kids Love*

Photography: Maren Caruso: p. 2, 11, 50, 53, 116, 130; Ben Fink: p. 26, 28, 39, 42, 58, 62, 68, 79, 83, 88, 93; JohnsonRauhoff: p. ii, vi, 17, 19, 32, 41, 44, 45, 47, 72, 76, 87, 95, 97, 106, 109, 125, 127, 128, 130; iStock: p. 7, 23, 81, 91, 100, 111, 113, 115

Design: Holly Ogden

www.andrewsmcmeel.com
www.surlatable.com

. . . .

ATTENTION: SCHOOLS AND BUSINESSES

Andrews McMeel books are available at quantity discounts with bulk purchase for educational, business, or sales promotional use. For information, please write to: Special Sales Department, Andrews McMeel Publishing, LLC, 1130 Walnut Street, Kansas City, Missouri 64106.

Introduction

"Comfort food" might be described as the best things about childhood in edible form—soothing soups, savory casseroles, homemade cakes, pies, and creamy puddings. It's the kind of food that goes right to your soul and gives you a bit of tasty refuge from the stresses of the day.

The great thing about comfort food is that you don't actually need to have had an idyllic mom-in-a-flowered-apron childhood to get all the delicious benefit of it. Even if your kitchen memories include more beeps from the microwave than sizzle of fried chicken in a skillet, you can create that nurturing and nourishing world yourself in your own kitchen.

Gathered inside this book are many of those must-have family dishes: strawberry shortcake, chicken noodle soup, meat loaf. But we don't think that comfort food should be pure nostalgia. After all, tastes have changed, ingredients are better now . . . and frankly, lots of our mothers and grandmothers weren't actually such great cooks!

That's why these recipes are both comforting *and* contemporary, keeping the soulfulness of true comfort food but adding more excitement and sophistication. The ingredient lists include fresh herbs, exotic spices, extra-virgin olive oil, dried mushrooms, balsamic vinegar—not ingredients likely to have been in your mother's pantry but definitely in your own.

Plain mashed potatoes become Roasted Garlic Mashed Potatoes; beef stew is now Beef Stew with Zinfandel and Dried Porcini Sauce. Burgers are stuffed with cheese and topped with caramelized red onion; simple chili gets jazzed with a chipotle cream; go way beyond chocolate sauce and serve our old-fashioned ice cream sundae with roasted pineapple and salted caramel sauce. Same comfort, new style.

Some of the recipes are quick-to-make hits of happiness, such as the Grilled Cheese Sandwich or Buttermilk Biscuits, while others require a few hours of lazy simmering or roasting, such as Fragrant Asian Beef Noodle Soup—the scents filling the house become part of the pleasure of the dish. There's something here for everyone who wants to cook, eat, and share meals that please both your body and your soul.

Sweet Breads

Soft and Sweet
Cinnamon Rolls

MAKES 8 ROLLS

Warm, tender cinnamon rolls, fresh from the oven, make a delectable treat any time of day. The aromas of cinnamon and freshly baked bread will have everyone waiting with anticipation. Freshly glazed, chock-full of cinnamon with a sticky, sweet topping, these spiral buns will leave your stomach cheering for more.

1   To make the dough, pour ¼ cup of the warm milk in a small bowl. Add the yeast and granulated sugar and stir to dissolve. Set the bowl aside for 8 to 10 minutes, until the mixture looks foamy. If the yeast isn't foamy after 15 minutes, start with a new package.

2   Put the flour and salt in a large bowl and whisk to blend. Make a well in the center, and pour the yeasted milk into the well. Then add the remaining 1 cup warm milk and melted butter. Stir together the ingredients until you get big, shaggy clumps of dough that start to stick together.

3   Sprinkle a little flour on your work surface. You can always add more later, so don't sprinkle too much. Dump the dough clumps out of the bowl onto your work surface. Dip your hands in flour and start kneading the dough. Using the heel of both hands, firmly push the top of the mound away from you. Fold the far side of the dough toward you, then rotate the mound of

....

Ingredients

Dough

1¼ cups warm milk (no hotter than 120°F)

1 tablespoon active dry yeast, or 2¼ teaspoons quick-rise yeast

2 teaspoons granulated sugar

3¼ cups unbleached all-purpose flour, plus more for sprinkling

1½ teaspoons salt

4 tablespoons (½ stick) unsalted butter, melted

1 large egg yolk

1 teaspoon water

Filling

1½ cups lightly packed light brown sugar

1½ tablespoons ground cinnamon

1 large egg

Icing

1 cup powdered sugar, or a little more if needed

1½ tablespoons water

....

dough a quarter turn and push again. Keep kneading until you get a smooth, springy dough. It usually takes 8 to 10 minutes. To know if you have kneaded enough, press your hand into the dough and remove it quickly. Your handprint should bounce back and disappear quickly. If it doesn't, keep kneading.

4   Lightly flour your hands and the surface if the dough starts sticking. It should feel tacky, like tape, but not sticky and gooey. A bench scraper is handy for scraping up any bits of dough stuck to the table and to help you move the dough around.

5   Rub the inside of a large bowl with a thin layer of vegetable oil or coat with pan spray. Shape the dough into a ball and put it in the bowl. Lightly rub or spray the top of the dough with a little oil. Cover the bowl with plastic wrap. Set the bowl aside and let the dough rise for 45 to 60 minutes, until it is twice as big.

6   While the bread dough finishes rising, make the filling. Put the brown sugar and cinnamon in a medium bowl and whisk together until well blended. Smash any brown sugar lumps to break them up. Crack the egg into a small bowl and beat with a fork until blended.

7   To roll out the dough, sprinkle 3 tablespoons flour on the work surface. Turn the risen dough out of the bowl onto the floured

surface and shape it into a rough rectangle. Sprinkle another tablespoon of flour on top. Starting from the edge closest to you, roll gently but firmly to the edge opposite you and then back again twice. Be careful not to roll the pin off the edge of the dough, or the dough will stick to the surface. Turn the dough a quarter turn, and roll up and back again twice. When you turn the dough, it should move easily. If it doesn't, gently lift the area of stuck dough, loosening it with the small metal spatula, and sprinkle some more flour underneath. Repeat the rolling up and back and turning of the dough until you have a 15 by 12-inch rectangle.

8   Brush any excess flour from the top and bottom of the dough with the large brush, and clean up any extra flour from around the dough with the bench scraper. Position the rectangle so you are facing a long side. Mix the egg yolk with the water and then, using a small pastry brush, brush a thin coating of the egg mixture all over the top of the dough. (You won't need all of it.) Use your fingers to scrape the filling onto the dough and spread it evenly over the surface, leaving a 1-inch-wide border uncovered along the long side opposite you. Starting at the long side closest to you, roll up the dough into a log, keeping it fairly tight as you go. When you reach the opposite side, roll the dough right on top of the uncovered border. Roll the log backward,

so the seam is on top, and pinch all along the seam to seal it.

9   Lightly butter a 10 by 2-inch cake pan or spray with pan spray. Using a serrated knife, cut the log crosswise into 10 rolls, each about 1½ inches wide. Use a gentle sawing motion when you cut so you don't flatten the log. Arrange the rolls in the prepared cake pan evenly, spacing 8 rolls around the edge of the pan and putting 2 rolls in the center.

10 Cover the pan with plastic wrap and set in a warm place. Let the rolls rise for about 1 hour, or until they are nearly twice as big and fill almost all of the open spaces in the pan. After the rolls have risen for about 30 minutes, position an oven rack in the center of the oven and preheat the oven to 350°F. That way the oven will be ready when you are ready to bake.

11 Bake the rolls for 30 to 35 minutes, until they are golden and the sugar is bubbling around the edges. Using oven mitts, transfer the pan to a cooling rack. Let cool for 10 to 15 minutes.

12 To make the icing, put 1 cup powdered sugar in a small bowl. Add the water and whisk until well blended and completely smooth. The icing should be thick, because it thins out when it hits the warm rolls. If it is thin and runny, add a little more sugar. Using the spoon, drizzle the icing over the tops of the warm rolls in any pattern you like. Eat them while they are warm.

Easy Morning Muffins
with Raspberries

MAKES 12 MUFFINS

Soft-crumbed and as comforting as a hug when warm from the oven, these muffins are perfect for home bakers too sleepy to pull out an electric mixer in the morning. Simply combine the dry ingredients in one bowl, the liquid in another, then mix the two and fold in the raspberries. If you measure everything out the night before, these can be tossed together in no time, even on a weekday morning. They're a great project for kids.

1   Preheat the oven to 400°F and position an oven rack in the center. Lightly coat a standard 12-cup muffin pan with melted butter, oil, or high-heat canola oil spray. Place the flour, ⅔ cup of the sugar, the baking powder, baking soda, and salt in a large bowl. Whisk to blend thoroughly.

2   In a medium skillet, melt the butter with the lemon zest (this will help to bring out the flavor of the zest and distribute it evenly in the batter). Turn off the heat. Add the buttermilk and let it sit for 1 to 2 minutes, just until it is tepid. Pour the liquid into a medium bowl, and add the eggs and vanilla. Whisk until well blended.

3   Make a well in the center of the dry ingredients. Pour the liquid ingredients into the well. Mix only until there are no more streaks of flour or pools of liquid and the batter looks smooth.

A few small lumps scattered throughout are fine—they will disappear during baking. Gently fold in the raspberries until evenly distributed.

4   Use a large ice-cream scoop or 2 soupspoons to divide the batter evenly into the prepared muffin cups. Stir together the remaining 1 tablespoon sugar and the cinnamon and sprinkle it over the tops of the muffins.

5   Bake the muffins for 18 to 20 minutes, until the tops feel firm and a skewer inserted into the centers comes out clean. Transfer the muffin pan to a rack and let cool for 5 minutes. Gently run a knife or spatula around each muffin to free it from the pan, lift the muffins out, and transfer them to the rack to finish cooling (careful, these are tender while hot). Serve warm or at room temperature.

Cinnamon-Streusel
Sour Cream Coffee Cake

There's a reason this coffee cake is an American classic. Its velvet crumb and generous layers of cinnamon streusel both inside and out make it a supreme indulgence on a lazy weekend morning. The touch of cocoa powder in the streusel tempers the sweetness and adds a subtle depth of flavor—you won't notice it's there, but it gives the topping a little extra *oomph*. Standing tall and beautifully brown, the cake's striking presence on the brunch table is like a magnet for family and friends. Also, it's a real keeper because it will be delicious and moist for at least 3 to 4 days after baking. Cakes like this one freeze beautifully, so you can even make it up to a month in advance. The best accompaniments are a bowl of fresh fruit and a cup of good coffee. Oh, and don't forget the Sunday paper.

The cake will keep at room temperature for up to 4 days covered with plastic wrap or a cake dome. Once it has been cut, press a piece of plastic wrap against the cut edges to keep the interior fresh. The cake can be frozen, double wrapped in plastic, for up to 4 weeks. Thaw, still wrapped in plastic to avoid condensation, for 3 hours before serving. Remove the plastic, wrap in aluminum foil, and reheat in a 325°F oven for 20 minutes, or until warmed through.

1   Preheat the oven to 350°F and position an oven rack in the lower third. Lightly coat a 10-inch tube pan with a removable bottom with melted butter, oil, or high-heat canola oil spray, dust it with flour, and tap out the excess.

2 To make the streusel, place the brown sugar, cinnamon, and cocoa powder in a medium bowl and stir with a spoon until well blended. Smash any lumps of brown sugar or cocoa so the mixture is even in texture. Add the pecans and stir to blend.

3 Place the flour, baking powder, baking soda, and salt in a medium bowl and whisk to blend thoroughly.

4 Put the butter and granulated sugar in the bowl of a stand mixer and beat on medium-high speed until the mixture is very light, almost white in color, 4 to 5 minutes. You can also use a hand mixer and a medium bowl, though you may need to beat the mixture a little longer to achieve the same results. Scrape down the bowl with a spatula.

5 Crack the eggs into a small bowl and beat with a fork to blend. Add the vanilla and beat well. With the mixer running on medium, add the eggs to the butter mixture about 1 tablespoon at a time, blending well after each addition. About halfway through, turn off the mixer and use the spatula to scrape down the bowl; then continue using the rest of the eggs. Scrape down the bowl again.

6 With the mixer running on the lowest speed, add one-third of the dry ingredients. Just as it is barely blended and you can still see a few patches of flour, add half of the sour cream.

Repeat, ending with the dry ingredients. Scrape down the bowl and finish blending the batter by hand.

7 Spoon half of the batter into a 10-inch tube pan with a removable bottom, and smooth the top. Sprinkle half of the streusel evenly over the batter. Spoon the remaining batter into the pan and level and smooth the top. Sprinkle the remaining streusel over the top. Bake for 65 to 75 minutes, until the cake is firm to the touch and a skewer inserted into the center comes out clean. Transfer to a rack to cool for at least 30 minutes if you want to serve it warm, or about 1½ hours to cool completely.

8 Run a thin knife or spatula around the inner tube of the pan to loosen the cake. Lift the center portion of the pan, with the cake, out of the ring. Run a thin knife or spatula around the bottom of the cake to release it from the bottom of the pan, Hold the cake firmly with your hands on both sides. Gently lift the cake, sliding it up the tube portion until it comes completely off the pan. Set it on a serving plate. Use a serrated knife to cut slices.

Banana Chocolate Chip Bread

with Chocolate Icing

MAKES 1 (9 BY 5-INCH) LOAF

Banana bread becomes so much less ordinary when paired with chocolate icing and chocolate chips. Chocolate and bananas have been a terrific dessert combo since the advent of banana splits with chocolate sauce and frozen bananas dipped in chocolate. This recipe will drive your stomach bananas.

1   Preheat the oven to 350°F and position an oven rack in the center of the oven. Lightly butter a 9 by 5-inch loaf pan, or spray with pan spray.

2   Peel the bananas and break them into pieces in a medium bowl. Using a fork or potato masher, smash them into pulp. It's okay if a few small lumps of banana remain. You should have about 1½ cups banana pulp.

3   Put the flour, baking soda, and salt in a large bowl and whisk to blend well. Add the eggs, sugar, oil, and vanilla to the banana pulp and whisk to blend well. Make a well in the center of the dry ingredients, and pour the mashed banana into the well. Whisk until the batter is smooth and you don't see any more patches of flour. Gently stir in the chocolate chips.

4 Scrape the batter into the prepared loaf pan and smooth the top. Bake for 65 to 75 minutes, until deep golden brown, firm to the touch in the center, and a toothpick inserted into the center comes out clean. You may see some melted chocolate on the toothpick from the chocolate chips. Using oven mitts, transfer the pan to the cooling rack and let the bread cool completely.

5 To make the icing, put the chocolate pieces in a medium bowl. Pour the cream into a small saucepan and place over medium heat, just until it begins to boil. Turn off the heat, and immediately pour the cream over the chocolate. Let it sit for 2 minutes, then whisk gently until blended and smooth. Let cool for 5 to 10 minutes, until the icing runs off the tip of a teaspoon like warm honey.

6 Remove the cake from the pan by turning it upside down and firmly shaking the pan a couple of times, while guiding the cake out onto your hand. Turn the cake right side up on a serving plate or a piece of parchment paper. Using a tablespoon, spoon the icing evenly over the top, letting some of it drip down the sides. Let the icing set for 20 minutes before slicing. Or leave the cake, uncovered, at room temperature until serving time.

Savory Breads

Old-Fashioned
Dinner Rolls

MAKES 9 OR 10 ROLLS

Bakers have been using potatoes (and potato cooking water) for many years. Yeast loves the starchy carbohydrates in potatoes. Their lumpy texture adds not only flavor and moisture, but also a chewy softness that is ideal in dinner rolls. Serve these at a family dinner and watch them disappear. The recipe can be doubled for a holiday dinner.

The rolls will keep, uncovered at room temperature, for 1 day. For longer storage, double wrap each in plastic, put in a large resealable plastic freezer bag, and freeze for up to 3 weeks. Thaw on the counter for 1½ hours, or until they reach room temperature. To reheat, remove from the plastic, wrap in aluminum foil, and return to a 375°F oven for 5 to 7 minutes, until warmed through.

1   Put the quartered potato in a small saucepan, cover with water, and set over medium heat. Bring to a simmer and cook for 15 to 20 minutes, until the tip of a paring knife slides in and out easily. Drain well, reserving ¼ cup of the cooking water. Return the potato to the pan and mash using a potato masher or fork. Set aside to cool to room temperature.

2   Warm the potato water to 110° to 115°F and pour into the bowl of a stand mixer. Add the yeast and 1 teaspoon of the sugar and whisk by hand to blend. Allow the mixture to sit for 10 minutes, or until the yeast is activated and foamy or bubbling. Measure ¼ cup mashed potatoes and add to the bowl. Add the remaining sugar, butter, milk, and egg and whisk by hand

until well blended. Add the flour and salt and knead on low speed for 2 to 3 minutes, until the dough comes together. It will seem sticky. With the mixer on low, add additional flour, a tablespoon at a time, until the dough pulls away from the sides of the bowl. Turn the speed to medium-low and continue to knead until the dough feels firm, dense, and springy, 5 to 6 minutes. Note: This dough is soft and sticky and will not pull away from the sides completely. Do not overknead or the starch from the potato will break down and make the dough gooey.

3   Lightly butter or oil a bowl and scrape the dough into it. Lightly coat the surface of the dough with a little butter or oil. Cover with plastic wrap or a damp lint-free cotton towel and let the dough rise until doubled in size, 45 to 60 minutes (longer if the room is cold).

4   Turn the dough out onto a lightly floured work surface. Press down on the dough firmly to expel some of the air bubbles. Chill, covered, for at least 2 hours and up to overnight, or until the dough is very cold.

5   Line a baking sheet with parchment paper or a silicone mat. Cut the dough into ⅓-cup

portions and shape each into a taut, round ball. Press the dough into a flattened disk, then grab the edges and draw them up into the center, pinching all the edges together where they meet. Flip the dough over so the smooth side is up. Cup your hands around the dough and create extra tension by gently pulling the dough downward and tucking it under. Move the dough in a small circle between your cupped hands, passing it back and forth, and gently tucking around the edges to create extra tension. Position the rolls on the baking sheet about 3 inches apart.

6   Cover the rolls loosely with plastic wrap or a damp lint-free cotton towel and let rise until almost doubled in size, 35 to 40 minutes (longer if the room is cold).

7   Preheat the oven to 375°F and position an oven rack in the middle of the oven. Bake the rolls for 10 minutes. Rotate the pan and continue to bake for 10 to 15 minutes longer, until the rolls are golden brown and their internal temperature registers 200°F on an instant-read thermometer. Transfer to a cooling rack. Serve warm or at room temperature.

Herb Corn Bread

MAKES 1 (9 BY 5-INCH) LOAF

This might be a simple quick bread, but the addition of fresh herbs and summer corn takes it to a whole new level. Don't substitute dried herbs here—they won't give you the dynamic flavor that fresh ones offer. This goes great with the Beef and Bean Chili with Chipotle Cream (page 31).

1   Preheat the oven to 350°F and position an oven rack in the center. Lightly coat a 9 by 5-inch loaf pan with melted butter or canola oil spray and line with a piece of parchment paper that extends 1 inch beyond the edge of both sides of the pan. In a medium bowl, whisk the flour, cornmeal, sugar, baking powder, salt, and pepper to blend well. Add the shallot, corn kernels, thyme, sage, and parsley. Whisk again to blend everything thoroughly.

2   In a second medium bowl or large measuring cup, whisk together the half-and-half and eggs. Make a well in the dry ingredients and pour the liquid ingredients into the well, then add the melted butter. Use a whisk to gently combine the ingredients, stirring just until the batter is homogenous and there are no patches of egg or flour. Don't overmix or the corn bread may be tunneled with holes.

3   Scrape the batter into the prepared loaf pan. Bake for 40 to 50 minutes, until the center of the bread feels firm to the touch and a skewer inserted into the center comes out clean. Transfer to a rack and let cool for 10 to 15 minutes before turning it out of the pan (it may also be left in the pan to cool completely). Peel off the parchment paper and cut into slices.

Parmesan-Herb
Popovers

Popovers' simple ingredients and mixing method belie the great heights to which they rise during baking, puffing up like crispy brown balloons. A classic popover pan is designed to optimize that rise, with tall narrow cups that force the batter upward. The recipe here gives instructions for baking popovers in a regular muffin pan. Although they don't rise as high when baked in a muffin pan, they develop a rounded depression at the bottom that, when turned upside down, is the perfect spot for sautéed mushrooms or a generous spoonful of soft-scrambled eggs. If you like, leave out the cheese and rosemary and fill the depression with your favorite jam.

1 Preheat the oven to 450°F and position an oven rack in the center. Lightly coat a standard 12-cup muffin pan with melted butter, oil, or high-heat canola oil spray. Once the oven is fully heated, heat the prepared muffin pan in the oven for 7 minutes.

2 In a medium bowl, whisk together the milk, eggs, melted butter, flour, and salt until well blended. Add the cheese and rosemary and blend well.

3 Scrape the batter into a large measuring cup. Remove the hot pan from the oven and divide the batter evenly among the prepared cups. Return the pan to the oven and bake for 15 minutes. Turn the oven down to 400°F and continue to bake for 15 minutes longer, until the popovers are puffed and deep golden brown. Cool the pan on a rack for a couple of minutes. Remove the popovers with a spoon. Serve hot.

Variation: For classic popovers, use a classic popover pan. The deep wells in the pan will need more batter, so you'll need to double the recipe. Omit the Parmesan cheese and rosemary and increase the salt to ½ teaspoon. Bake for 20 minutes at 450°F, then lower the oven temperature to 350°F and continue to bake for 15 to 18 minutes, until the popovers are a deep golden brown. Serve immediately.

Pizza Margherita

MAKES 1 (12-INCH) PIZZA

Pizza is a hands-down favorite anytime, anywhere. And while you can get good pizza when eating out, truly great pizza is much easier to find at home, mostly because you can top it exactly the way you want. The Margherita is the simplest of all pizzas, a classic tomato and cheese, representing the colors of the Italian flag with a green sprinkling of fresh basil. The dough can be stored in the refrigerator for 24 hours or frozen for up to 1 month. To help it slide onto the pizza stone or upturned pan, dust with semolina. If you don't have semolina, cornmeal will work, but it burns more quickly.

1   Pour the warm water into the bowl of a stand mixer. Add the yeast, whisk by hand to blend, and allow to sit for 5 to 10 minutes, until the yeast is activated and looks creamy. Add the ½ cup water and 4 teaspoons olive oil and whisk by hand to blend. Add the flour and salt. Knead the dough on low speed for 2 minutes, or until it comes together in a cohesive mass. Cover the bowl with plastic wrap or a damp lint-free cotton towel and let the dough rest for 20 minutes to allow it to fully hydrate before further kneading. Turn the mixer to medium-low and continue to knead until the dough is firm, elastic, and smooth, 3 to 6 minutes.

2   Lightly oil a bowl and scrape the dough into it, then lightly coat the surface of the dough with a little oil. Cover tightly with plastic wrap and let the dough rise at room temperature until doubled, 45 to 60 minutes (longer if the room is cold).

3 Place a pizza stone or overturned sheet pan in the oven. Preheat the oven to 500°F. Allow 30 minutes to 1 hour for the stone to fully heat.

4 Turn the dough out onto a lightly floured work surface. Press down on the dough firmly to expel some of the air bubbles, but don't knead the dough again or it will be too springy and difficult to shape (if this happens, simply cover the dough with plastic wrap or a damp lint-free cotton towel and let it rest for 10 to 15 minutes to give the gluten some time to relax).

5 Dust the top of the dough with flour, then press down with your fingers (or use a rolling pin) to flatten the dough into a disk about 12 inches in diameter. Alternatively, slip your hands, knuckles up, under the dough and lift it up, then gently stretch the dough by pulling your fists apart. Rotate the dough each time you pull so the dough is stretched into an even circle. Brush any excess flour from the surface and underside of the dough.

6 Center the round of dough on a piece of parchment paper on top of a sheet pan. Spread the tomato sauce over the pizza dough, leaving a ½-inch border. Slice the mozzarella as thinly as possible (at least ¼ inch—a serrated knife works well here), or grate it. Arrange the cheese over the sauce.

7 Shake the sheet forward and back to make sure the pizza is loose enough to slide. If it's stuck, use a spatula to lift up the dough and toss a bit of semolina underneath. Once the pizza moves freely, gently shake the sheet until the pizza is at the very front edge. Open the oven door and set the front edge of the sheet at the back of the baking stone or upturned sheet pan. With a quick jerk, let the pizza settle on the stone or pan. Bake for 7 to 9 minutes, until the dough is golden brown at the edges and across the bottom.

8 Transfer the pizza to a cutting board. Brush the edges with the 1 tablespoon olive oil to give the golden crust a beautiful shine. Scatter the basil over the top and cut the pizza into 8 wedges. Serve immediately.

Buttermilk Biscuits

MAKES 8 BISCUITS

It should take no time for you to whip up a bunch of these fluffy, tender biscuits to serve for breakfast, lunch, or supper. In fact, the dough goes together so quickly that you can wait until the oven is fully preheated before you start mixing it.

1 Position a rack in the center of the oven and preheat the oven to 425°F. Line a baking sheet with parchment paper or a silicone baking mat.

2 In a bowl, stir together the flour, baking powder, baking soda, and salt. Scatter the butter over the top and mix with a fork to coat the pieces. Using a pastry blender or two butter knives, cut the butter into the flour, scraping off any butter pieces. Continue cutting until the dough resembles a combination of crushed crackers and pea-sized butter pieces. Pour in the buttermilk and stir with a fork just until the batter holds together in a mass. Don't worry if there are dried bits of flour on the bottom of the bowl.

3 Turn the dough out onto a lightly floured work surface and gently knead just until it holds together. Pat the dough into a 7-inch round about 1 inch thick. Cut the dough with a biscuit cutter or water glass into 2½-inch circles. Transfer the rounds to the prepared baking sheet, spacing them about 2 inches apart. Repeat until all the dough is used up. Brush the tops with a thin coating of the beaten egg (you will not use all the egg).

4 Bake for 14 to 17 minutes, until firm to the touch and golden brown. Transfer the biscuits to a rack and let cool for at least 5 minutes. Serve warm or at room temperature.

Soups, Stews, and Sandwiches

Kabocha Squash Soup

with Toasted Cumin and Chiles

SERVES 4 TO 6

The Japanese kabocha squash is squat and round, and has nubby, dark green skin and dense, sweet flesh. Use a large, heavy chef's knife to cut the squash into big chunks. Because the skin is too thick and brittle to peel, the squash is cooked and then the flesh is scooped from the skin. Pureed with coconut milk, it makes a rich, golden soup. Balance the richness with a generous addition of fresh lime juice, slivered chiles, and a shower of chopped cilantro.

1   In a large pot with a steamer insert, steam the squash for 20 minutes, or until tender when pierced with a fork. Remove to a cutting board and cool.

2   Wipe the pot dry. Add the oil, place over medium heat, and heat the oil until hot enough to sizzle a piece of onion. Add the onion and cook over low heat, stirring with a wooden spoon, for 3 minutes, or until the onion is translucent. Stir in the garlic and cook for 30 seconds. Add the cumin and cook, stirring, for 1 minute. Remove from the heat.

3   Scoop the cooled squash from the brittle skins and add it to the pot. Stir in the coconut milk.

4   Puree the soup with an immersion blender or in batches in a blender. Add the salt and pepper.

Ingredients

- 1 (4-pound) kabocha squash, cut into large chunks, seeds and membranes removed
- 1 tablespoon vegetable oil
- ½ cup chopped yellow onion
- 1 clove garlic, minced or grated
- 2½ teaspoons ground cumin
- 2 (14-ounce) cans light or regular coconut milk
- 2 teaspoons coarse salt
- ¼ teaspoon freshly ground black pepper
- ¼ cup fresh lime juice
- 1 red or green jalapeño chile, halved lengthwise, seeded, and slivered crosswise
- 2 tablespoons chopped fresh cilantro

5 Reheat the soup over medium-low heat, stirring to prevent sticking, until steaming. Do not allow to boil. Stir in the lime juice, half of the chile, and 1 tablespoon of the cilantro. Taste and adjust the seasoning with salt. Ladle into warmed bowls. Garnish with the remaining chile and the remaining tablespoon of cilantro.

Ingredients

Broth and Chicken

1 (4-pound) whole chicken

2 pounds chicken backs and necks

2 quarts low-sodium chicken broth

1 large carrot, peeled and
  quartered crosswise

1 stalk celery, quartered crosswise

1 yellow onion, quartered

6 cloves garlic

2 leafy sprigs Italian parsley

1 stem thyme

2 whole cloves

6 black peppercorns

Coarse salt

2 medium carrots, peeled and cut
  into ¼-inch slices

2 medium stalks celery, cut into
  ¼-inch slices

1 medium turnip, peeled and cut
  into small dice

8 ounces dried egg noodles

¼ cup chopped fresh Italian
  parsley

Rich and Comforting
Chicken Noodle Soup

SERVES 6

It may seem crazy, but we're giving our from-scratch chicken broth a boost by making it with both water and some canned broth. A truly great chicken soup is all about the broth, and we find that some modern chickens just don't have enough flavor to produce a rich enough soup. You can use all water if you prefer, but be sure to add enough salt to the finished soup to make it truly savory.

1   To make the broth and cook the chicken, put all the chicken in a large pot, and add the broth and enough water to cover, about 1½ more quarts. Add the carrot, celery, onion, garlic, parsley, thyme, cloves, peppercorns, and 2 teaspoons salt to the pot. Set the pot over low heat, cover, and heat slowly until just barely simmering. Uncover and watch the pot. As foam rises to the top, skim it off with a fine-mesh strainer or perforated spoon.

2   Cook the chicken in the barely simmering water over low heat for about 40 minutes, or until very tender. Remove the chicken, set aside until cool enough to handle, then pull the skin off the meat, reserving the skin. Pull or cut the cooked chicken from the bones into bite-sized pieces and keep refrigerated until ready to serve the soup. Add the bones and gristle and the reserved skin back to the broth. Continue to simmer,

uncovered, over low heat for 2 hours longer, or until the broth is reduced to about 2½ quarts.

3   Remove the pot from the heat and let the broth stand for 1 to 2 hours, until lukewarm. Line a fine-mesh strainer with cheesecloth and place over a large bowl. Strain the broth and discard the solids.

4   If there isn't room in the refrigerator for the bowl of broth, divide it among smaller containers. Cover and refrigerate for several hours or overnight until well chilled and the fat has solidified on the surface. Lift of the fat with a spoon or sieve. (The broth will keep, covered, in the refrigerator for up to 3 days or in the freezer for up to 4 months.)

5   To assemble the soup, put the defatted broth back into a large pot and bring to a simmer. Bring another large pot of generously salted water to a boil. Add the carrots, celery, and turnip and cook until just tender, about 5 minutes. Scoop out with a perforated spoon or Chinese skimmer and add to the simmering broth.

6   Add the noodles to the boiling water and cook until al dente. Drain well and add to the simmering broth, along with the cooked reserved chicken meat. After a few minutes, taste and adjust the salt level. Serve in shallow bowls, with parsley sprinkled on top.

Beef and Bean Chili

with Chipotle Cream

SERVES 4 TO 6

We're not even going to touch the debate about what constitutes "real" chili. We just know that this easy-to-make, family-friendly version is hearty and delicious. The generous measure of beans makes it super healthful, too. Fresh chiles and chili powder add a moderate amount of heat, but you can raise the bar a bit with the chipotle cream, adding a little or a lot of heat, to your taste.

1   Heat 1 tablespoon of the oil in a large heavy-based saucepan or Dutch oven over medium-high heat. Add the beef, season with 2 teaspoons of the salt, and cook, stirring frequently, until the meat has lost its pink color, about 5 minutes. Don't let the beef actually brown. Scrape the meat from the pan to a strainer set over a bowl and drain.

2   Add the rest of the oil to the pan. Toss in the onions and 1 more teaspoon salt. Reduce the heat to medium and cook, stirring frequently, until the onions are soft and fragrant, 4 to 5 minutes. Add the Anaheim chiles and continue cooking until all the vegetables are soft and just starting to brown around the edges, another 8 to 10 minutes. Add the garlic, chili powder, smoked paprika, and cumin and cook for another minute, stirring and scraping so the spices fry slightly in the oil.

Ingredients

- ¼ cup olive oil
- 2 pounds ground beef (80 to 85% lean, if possible)
- 1½ tablespoons coarse salt, or more to taste
- 2 cups chopped yellow onions
- 2 medium Anaheim or other mild medium chiles, seeded and chopped
- 5 cloves garlic, minced
- 2 tablespoons mild chili powder
- 1 tablespoon smoked paprika
- 1 tablespoon ground cumin
- 2 (28-ounce) cans whole peeled tomatoes with juices
- 2 (15-ounce) cans pinto beans, rinsed and drained
- 6 (4-inch) stems cilantro
- 1 cup low-sodium beef broth
- 2 tablespoons molasses (optional)
- ½ cup sour cream or Mexican crema
- 1 teaspoon adobo sauce from a can of chipotle chiles, or more to taste (freeze the leftover sauce and chiles for later use)
- ½ cup chopped fresh cilantro leaves
- 6 lime wedges

3 Add the tomatoes and their juices, breaking them up into bite-sized pieces with a wooden spoon or a potato masher. Add the beans, cilantro stems, beef broth, molasses (if using), and remaining teaspoon salt. Stir together, reduce the heat to low, and simmer, uncovered, until thickened and rich tasting, 45 to 55 minutes. Add back the beef and simmer for another 15 minutes. Taste and adjust the salt and spices.

4 Stir the sour cream and adobo sauce together, taste, and adjust the heat level. Serve the chile in bowls with a spoonful of the cream and chopped cilantro on top and a wedge of lime on the side.

Fragrant

Asian Beef Noodle Soup

SERVES 6

The goodness of this soup depends almost entirely on the broth, so it pays to take your time and let the broth simmer lazily until the flavors are deep and rich. Your house will smell so good that you may just want to have a pot of this on your stove all the time! To get a truly grease-free broth, you'll want to make the broth a day ahead so you can chill it, letting the fat float to the top and harden for easy scooping off.

1   To make the broth, put all the bones and ribs in a large pot (at least 12 quarts), cover with water, and bring to a boil. Let everything boil for a couple of minutes, then drain the water. Refill with about 4 quarts water and bring to a simmer.

2   Meanwhile, char the onions and ginger by either holding them over a gas flame until deep brown and charred, or placing them, cut side down, in a cast-iron skillet and cooking until very deeply browned, 3 to 5 minutes. Add the onions and ginger to the pot of broth, along with the fish sauce and sugar.

3   Simmer the broth, skimming any foam that forms on the surface, until the ribs are tender, about 2 hours. With tongs or a skimmer, remove the ribs, let cool, then cut or pick off the tasty meat and refrigerate until ready to serve the soup. Return everything else, including any fat or gristly bits, to the broth. Add the star anise, cinnamon stick, cloves, peppercorns, and

Ingredients

3 pounds beef marrow bones or other good soup bones

4 pounds meaty beef ribs or oxtails

2 small onions, halved

2 (3-inch) knobs fresh ginger, split lengthwise

¼ cup fish sauce, or more to taste

3 tablespoons sugar

6 whole star anise (or the equivalent in broken pieces)

1 (2-inch) cinnamon stick

6 whole cloves

10 whole black peppercorns

1 tablespoon coarse salt, or more to taste

8 ounces dried rice sticks or thin rice noodles

1 pound thick rib eye, sirloin, or tenderloin steak, fat trimmed, very thinly sliced (⅛ inch)

6 to 8 ounces mung bean sprouts, rinsed and drained

½ cup lightly packed fresh cilantro leaves, coarsely chopped, plus more for the table

Hot sauce for garnish

1½ limes, cut into quarters (to yield 6), for garnish

the salt and continue simmering until deeply flavorful, another 1½ to 3 hours.

4   Fish out all the bones and large spices (especially the star anise, which can get strong) and discard them, then skim off as much fat as possible (if you can, make this ahead so you can cool the broth and skim off the hardened fat). Taste the broth and continue reducing to concentrate the flavors if necessary. You should end up with about 10 cups. Season with a bit more fish sauce and salt to make it strongly flavored.

5   Meanwhile, soak the rice sticks in cool water until softened, about 30 minutes. Bring a large pot of water to a boil; when ready to serve the soup, plunge the rice sticks into the boiling water and cook until tender and heated through, about 30 seconds. Drain thoroughly, then distribute among 6 wide soup bowls. Divide the cooked beef rib meat among the bowls, too, then lay the strips of raw rib eye on top.

6   Get the broth piping hot and ladle it into the bowls, allowing it to cook the raw beef. Top each bowl with a handful of bean sprouts and a pinch of cilantro leaves. Put the fish sauce and hot sauce on the dinner table, along with a bowl of limes and more cilantro, so diners can add their own garnishes.

Beef Stew with Zinfandel

and Dried Porcini Sauce

SERVES 6

In this beef stew, the meat cubes are marinated in wine that has been simmered with sautéed aromatic vegetables, herbs, spices, and strips of orange zest, and then cooled. For the best flavor and texture, select well-marbled beef chuck and ask the butcher—or you can do it yourself—to cut the meat into large cubes (about 1½ inches). Although there is a long list of ingredients, the preparation can be done up to three days before serving. Not only will the flavors improve, but the slow-cooked juices will chill and all the fat will collect on the surface, where it can be easily removed and discarded. This is a great dish to serve to company.

1   Place the meat in a single layer on a rimmed sheet pan and sprinkle each piece generously on all sides with salt and pepper. Cover and refrigerate.

2   To make the marinade, heat a large skillet or sauté pan over medium heat until hot enough for a drop of water to sizzle on contact. Add 2 tablespoons of oil and swirl to coat. Add the chopped onion, carrot, celery, and garlic, decrease the heat to medium-low, and sauté, stirring, for 6 minutes, or until tender but not browned. Add the Zinfandel, parsley, 2 of the orange zest strips, bay leaves, thyme sprig, and cinnamon stick and bring to a boil. Decrease the heat to low and simmer, without

Ingredients

3 to 4 pounds well-marbled boneless beef chuck, excess fat trimmed and cut into 1½-inch cubes

Coarse salt and freshly ground black pepper

6 tablespoons extra-virgin olive oil

1 cup chopped yellow onion

½ cup peeled and chopped carrot

½ cup chopped celery

1 tablespoon chopped garlic

1 bottle Zinfandel

¼ cup chopped fresh Italian parsley

3 (3 by ½-inch) strips orange zest

2 bay leaves

1 leafy sprig thyme

1 cinnamon stick

1 cup (1 ounce) dried porcini mushrooms

2 cups water

2 (¼-inch-thick) slices lean slab or thick-cut bacon, cubed

1 yellow onion, cut into thin wedges

1 clove garlic, bruised with a knife

1 cup drained canned Italian plum tomatoes

12 large shallots, halved lengthwise

12 large cremini mushrooms, halved through the caps

1 leafy sprig Italian parsley

1 teaspoon fresh thyme leaves

······················

boiling, for 10 minutes. Remove from the heat and let cool to room temperature.

3   Place the beef in a large bowl and carefully add the cooled marinade. Arrange the beef so that it is totally covered by the marinade. Cover and refrigerate overnight.

4   Set a colander over a bowl and drain the meat. Reserve the strained marinade. Save the orange zest strips, bay leaves, thyme sprig, and cinnamon stick, but discard the other chopped vegetables. Pat each piece of meat dry with paper towels and spread out on a rimmed sheet pan. Add another sprinkling of salt and pepper.

5   Combine the porcini and water in a small saucepan, and bring to a boil. Remove from the heat, cover, and let stand for 20 minutes, or until softened.

6   While the mushrooms are soaking, heat a large ovenproof pot over medium heat. Add the bacon, decrease the heat to medium-low, and cook, stirring, for 5 minutes, or until evenly browned. Use a slotted spoon to transfer the bacon to a plate. Discard almost all of the fat, leaving only a thin film in the pot.

7   Add 2 tablespoons of olive oil to the pot and heat over medium-high heat until hot enough for a piece of meat to sizzle on contact. Decrease the heat to medium. Working in

batches, add the meat to the hot pan and sear, turning with tongs as necessary, for 3 to 5 minutes, until well browned on all sides. As each batch is ready, transfer it to a plate. When all of the meat has been browned, spoon off the excess fat from the pan and discard.

8   Strain the porcini through a fine strainer set over a small bowl and press on the mushrooms to expel the excess water. Coarsely chop the porcini. Save the porcini water.

9   If necessary, rearrange the oven racks to accommodate the large pot. Preheat the oven to 325°F.

10 Return the pot to medium heat and heat until hot. Add the onion wedges and garlic clove to the hot fat and sauté, stirring, for 5 minutes, or until golden. Add the tomatoes and break them into chunks with the side of a spoon. Add the reserved strained marinade, the chopped porcini and porcini liquid, and the orange zest strips, bay leaves, thyme sprig, and cinnamon stick reserved from the marinade. Bring to a boil over high heat. Remove from the heat and add the browned meat and any juices that accumulated on the plate. Sprinkle the bacon on top. Cover and place in the lower half of the oven.

11 Cook for 2½ hours, or until the meat is fork-tender. Halfway through the cooking time,

remove from the oven and carefully lift the lid to check on the liquid in the pot. It should be simmering. If it is boiling, lower the oven temperature to 300°F. When the meat is fork-tender, remove the pot from the oven and let stand, covered, for 5 minutes.

12 If preparing the stew ahead, use a slotted spoon to transfer the meat to a storage bowl. Cover the meat and refrigerate until ready to reheat. Refrigerate the juices separately; the fat will solidify on the surface. Just before serving, place the cold meat in a shallow baking dish and cover tightly with aluminum foil. Preheat the oven to 350°F. Place the meat in the oven for 30 minutes, or until hot. Lift off and discard the fat from the refrigerated juices. Pour the defatted juices into a saucepan and heat to boiling. Decrease the heat to low, cover, and keep warm until ready to serve. To finish the dish, proceed to step 15.

13 If serving the stew soon after it is cooked, transfer the meat to a deep, heatproof serving dish, cover with foil, and keep warm in the turned-off oven. Set a strainer over a bowl and pour the contents of the pan into the strainer. Remove the orange zest strips, bay leaves, thyme sprig, and cinnamon stick, and discard. Spoon the other solids in the strainer over the meat.

14 Pour the strained juices into a fat separator and let stand for about 10 minutes, or until the fat rises to the surface. Carefully pour off the juices into a small saucepan. Or let the juices stand in the bowl until the fat rises to the surface, skim off and discard the fat with a spoon, and pour the defatted juices into a small saucepan. Keep the juices warm over low heat.

15 Just before serving, heat a large skillet over medium-low heat and add the remaining 2 tablespoons of olive oil. Add the shallots, cut sides down, and sauté, turning with tongs as they brown, for 10 minutes, or until evenly browned. Push the shallots to one side of the skillet to continue cooking. Add the cremini mushrooms to the skillet and sauté, turning as necessary, for 5 minutes, or until the mushrooms are evenly browned and tender and the shallots are tender and browned. Sprinkle with salt and pepper.

16 Finely chop the parsley, thyme, and remaining orange zest strip together for a garnish.

17 Spoon the shallots and mushrooms on top of the meat. Spoon the hot juices over the meat and vegetables. Sprinkle with the garnish and serve at once.

Winter Vegetable Stew

with Moroccan Flavors

SERVES 6 TO 8

Eight different vegetables and such heady spices as cinnamon, cumin, and paprika all contribute to the flavor of this hearty stew. Feel free to add other vegetables, but avoid adding strongly flavored ones, such as cabbage, broccoli, or cauliflower, or any vegetables that won't benefit from the long cooking time. If you have preserved lemons on hand, mince them and sprinkle on top of the stew just before serving.

1 Combine the carrots, celery, raisins, garlic, leek, squash, potatoes, rutabagas, turnips, and olive oil in a large Dutch oven or other ovenproof pot. Add the tomatoes, cumin, paprika, and salt. Fold together until blended. Tuck in the cinnamon stick and bay leaf.

2 Cover and place in a cold oven. Turn the oven to 450°F. Bake without disturbing for 1¾ hours. Remove from the oven and let stand, covered, for 10 minutes. Sprinkle with the cilantro and preserved lemons, if using. Serve hot from the oven or at room temperature.

Tomato Soup

with Saffron Cream

Nothing is better on a cold day than a cup of warm tomato soup and a gooey grilled cheese sandwich. This silken tomato soup—the elegant texture the result of pushing the soup through a fine sieve—carries a haunting hint of saffron and a pleasant hit of black pepper. Ideally, this soup is made with fresh tomatoes, but canned tomatoes can be substituted.

1   Combine the olive oil, leek, carrot, and garlic in a large Dutch oven or saucepan, place over medium heat, and heat, stirring, for about 10 minutes, or until the vegetables begin to sizzle. Decrease the heat to low, cover, and cook for 15 minutes, or until the vegetables are softened but not browned.

2   Meanwhile, put the saffron threads in a small, dry skillet, place over low heat, and warm for about 1 minute. Remove from the heat.

3   When the vegetables are ready, add ½ teaspoon of the heated saffron threads to the pan and reserve the remaining saffron in the skillet for the garnish. Heat the saffron in the vegetables, stirring, for 1 minute. Add the tomatoes, broth, and salt, and bring to a boil. Adjust the heat to medium-low, cover, and cook for 30 minutes, stirring occasionally and breaking up the

tomatoes with the side of a spoon. Add the pepper, then taste and adjust the seasoning with salt.

4   While the soup is cooking, make the saffron cream garnish: Add ½ cup of the cream to the saffron remaining in the skillet, place over low heat, and heat, stirring, until the cream is hot. Remove from the heat, cover, and let stand until ready to serve.

5   Remove the soup from the heat and let cool for about 20 minutes. Working in batches, ladle the soup into a blender and process until smooth. Alternatively, use an immersion blender to puree the soup in the pot.

6   Set a fine-mesh strainer over a large, deep bowl. Ladle the soup into the strainer. Let stand for about 45 minutes. Press on the solids to extract as much flavor as possible. Scrape the puree from the outside of the strainer into the broth.

7   Rinse out the pot and return the soup to it. Gradually add the remaining ½ cup of cream to the soup, stirring gently with a whisk until blended. Reheat, whisking gently, over low heat. Stir in the lemon juice. Do not allow to boil. Taste and add more salt and pepper if needed. Ladle into warmed soup plates.

8   Strain the saffron through a fine-mesh strainer and drizzle a scant tablespoon of saffron cream into each bowl of soup. Serve at once.

Grilled Cheese Sandwich

SERVES 1

Rarely do so few ingredients create such a wonderfully satisfying thing to eat. It's all about the cooking method, which isn't grilling at all, but rather "griddling," or cooking on a flat hot surface. A cast-iron skillet is best, but any heavy frying pan will do if you don't have a true griddle. Cooking with a lid at first helps the cheese melt faster, so if your skillet doesn't have a lid, borrow one from another pan. Whether you prefer sharp or mild Cheddar, get a good-quality cheese. This is not the time, however, for rustic artisanal breads. A good, firm sliced white or wheat bread from a package gives you the best results.

1   Spread one side of each slice of bread with the butter, taking care not to tear the bread. Flip one slice so the buttered side is down, then distribute the cheese evenly over the surface. Put a second piece of bread on top, buttered side up.

2   Heat a heavy skillet over medium heat, place the sandwich in the pan, cover the pan with a lid, and cook until the underside is a rich golden brown, about 2 minutes. Remove the lid, flip the sandwich, and press it firmly with a spatula (but don't squash it). Cook until the second side is evenly browned as well and you can see the cheese melting inside, another 2 minutes. Serve immediately.

Ingredients

2 slices thin white or wheat bread

2 teaspoons softened salted butter

½ cup lightly packed shredded Cheddar cheese

Variations: To go beyond the classic, add tomato and mustard. Spread the nonbuttered sides of the bread with a thin layer of Dijon mustard and lay 2 or 3 thin slices of tomato on the cheese. Continue as for the classic sandwich.

Or try pear and aged Gouda. Gently sauté 2 or 3 thin slices ripe but firm pear in a little butter. Cool slightly. Assemble the sandwich, using aged Gouda instead of Cheddar. Lay the pear slices on the cheese, and season with salt, pepper, and about ¼ teaspoon chopped fresh thyme. Continue as for the classic sandwich.

Deconstructed
Bacon and Egg Breakfast Sandwich

SERVES 2

You'll need individual ovenproof bowls or ramekins for this dish, each with about a 12-ounce capacity. If they're a little big, that's okay. Feel free to add other ingredients to the mix—crumbled cooked sausage, diced ham, cooked shrimp, roasted red pepper—anything that would taste good with cheese and cream. And what doesn't taste good with cheese and cream?

1   Preheat the oven to 425°F. Put about one-quarter of the muffin pieces, bacon, tomatoes, and chiles in the bottom of each of two 12-ounce ovenproof ramekins or bowls. Gently set the eggs on top and season with salt and pepper. Distribute the remaining bacon, tomatoes, and chiles on top of the eggs, add the remaining muffin pieces, and pour the cream over the top. Sprinkle with the cheese. Let the ramekins sit for at least 15 minutes before baking so that the muffin pieces absorb the cream. Note: This can be assembled the night before baking; cover tightly and refrigerate. Add 1 to 2 minutes to the baking time.

2   Put the ramekins on a baking sheet so they're easier to move when hot. Bake until the cheese is melty and beginning to brown and the cream is bubbling and has mostly been absorbed, 14 to 15 minutes. Let rest for about 5 minutes before serving.

Main Dishes

Herbed
Chicken Potpie

SERVES 8

The announcement "chicken potpie for dinner!" is always greeted with cheers, and who doesn't need a few extra cheers? This savory favorite is easier than ever to make thanks to the roasted chicken and chopped vegetables available in most markets. The recipe can be made in individual pie pans or bowls as well, though you may need to prepare a double recipe of dough to ensure you have enough to top each serving. After Thanksgiving, use leftover turkey instead of chicken.

Any leftovers may be covered with plastic wrap and refrigerated for up to 4 days. Reheat in a 375°F oven for 15 to 20 minutes before serving.

1   To make the dough, place the butter pieces in a bowl or on a plate and freeze for at least 20 minutes. Refrigerate the water in a small measuring cup until needed.

2   Place the flour and salt in the bowl of a food processor. Process for 10 seconds to blend the ingredients. Add the frozen butter pieces and pulse 6 to 10 times (in 1-second bursts), until the butter and flour mixture looks like crushed crackers and peas.

3   Immediately transfer the butter-flour mixture to the large bowl. Sprinkle a tablespoon of the cold water over the mixture and "fluff" it, then add another and another, until 3 tablespoons have been added. Continue to fluff and stir 10 to 12 times. It will not be a cohesive dough at this point but a bowl of shaggy

Ingredients

Flaky Pie Dough

½ cup (1 stick) cold unsalted butter, cut into ½-inch pieces

3 to 4 tablespoons cold water

1¼ cups unbleached all-purpose flour

¼ teaspoon salt

Herbed Chicken Filling

6 tablespoons (¾ stick) unsalted butter

1 cup diced onion

½ cup diced celery

6 tablespoons unbleached all-purpose flour

4 cups homemade chicken stock or canned low-sodium chicken broth

½ cup peeled and diced carrot

1 tablespoon olive oil

10 ounces sliced mushrooms

1 pound cooked chicken meat, diced

1 cup frozen peas

1 tablespoon chopped fresh chives

1½ tablespoons finely chopped fresh Italian parsley

1½ teaspoons finely chopped fresh thyme

Coarse salt and freshly ground black pepper

1 large egg yolk

2 tablespoons milk or cream

crumbs and clumps of dough. Before bringing the dough together, test it for the correct moisture content. Take a handful and squeeze firmly. Open your hand. If the clump falls apart and looks dry, remove any large, moist clumps from the bowl; then add more water, a teaspoon at a time, sprinkling it over the top of the mixture and immediately stirring or mixing it in. Test again before adding any more water. Repeat, if needed. The dough is done when it holds together (even if a few small pieces fall off). If the butter feels soft and squishy, refrigerate before continuing. If the butter is still cold and firm, continue to the next step. (Note: Adding the liquid may also be done on low speed in a stand mixer fitted with the paddle attachment—add three-quarters of the liquid, test for moistness, then add the remaining liquid if needed.)

4   Turn the dough onto a work surface and knead gently 3 to 6 times. If it won't come together and looks very dry, return it to the bowl and add another teaspoon or two of water (one at a time), mixing in as above, and try again. Flatten the dough into a 6- or 7-inch disk, wrap in plastic or parchment paper, and refrigerate for 30 minutes. This allows time for the dough to hydrate fully and for the butter to firm up again.

5   If the dough has been refrigerated for more than 30 minutes, it may be very firm and hard and will crack if you try to roll it. Let it sit on the counter for 10 to 15 minutes until it is malleable but still cold. Dust your work surface generously with flour and set the disk on the flour. Dust the top with flour. Roll, turning the dough, until you've got a 14- to 15-inch circle. If at any point the dough becomes warm and sticky, gently fold it into quarters, unfold it onto a baking sheet, and refrigerate for 15 minutes, or until the butter is firm again.

6   Transfer the circle of pie or tart to a baking sheet and chill until ready to use.

7   To make the filling, melt the butter over medium heat in a medium saucepan. Add the onion and celery and cook, stirring occasionally, for 5 to 7 minutes, until softened. Remove the pan from the heat and whisk in the flour. Whisk vigorously to blend the flour with the vegetables and butter. Return to the heat and cook, whisking, for 2 to 3 minutes (do not let the flour brown). Remove the pan from the heat. Add about 1 cup of the stock and whisk until the mixture is smooth and pastelike. This is your only chance to remove any lumps of flour, so whisk thoroughly. Once the paste is smooth, whisk in the remaining stock. Add the carrot. Reduce the heat and simmer for 5 minutes. Remove from the heat.

8   Fill a large bowl halfway with ice and water. Heat the olive oil in a medium sauté pan over high heat. Add the mushrooms and cook, stirring every 2 to 3 minutes, until deep golden

brown, 10 to 12 minutes. Add the mushrooms to the filling along with the chicken, peas, chives, parsley, and thyme. Season to taste with salt and pepper. Set the saucepan into the bowl of ice water. Stir occasionally until the filling is cool. (Chilling the filling prevents the flaky pastry from melting when it's placed on top of the pie.) Scrape the filling into the pie pan.

9   Preheat the oven to 275°F and position an oven rack in the center. Brush the edge of the pie pan with a thin film of water. Transfer the dough to the pan, roll the edges to form a thick rope along the edge of the pan, then crimp or form a decorative border as desired. Any leftover pie dough can be used to make decorative designs, such as a chicken, on top of the piecrust. In a small bowl, beat the egg yolk with the milk and use a pastry brush to lightly glaze the surface of the pie. Bake for 40 to 45 minutes, until the filling is bubbling and the crust is golden brown and crisp. Transfer to a rack and let cool for 15 to 20 minutes. Serve hot, spooning the pie into wide, shallow bowls.

Roast Leg of Lamb
with Fennel Seeds and Rosemary Crust

SERVES 8 TO 10

This is a delicious excuse to learn to carve bone-in leg of lamb. For an instant side dish, toss some potatoes around the lamb while it's roasting. When it's time to carve, start on the side with the crust. If some falls off as you slice, that's okay—just scoop it onto each serving.

1   Preheat the oven to 375°F. In a food processor, combine the bread crumbs, pine nuts, rosemary, anchovies, garlic, and fennel seeds. Process until the nuts and garlic are finely chopped, 10 to 15 seconds. Add ½ cup of the olive oil, the mustard, a pinch of salt, and a few grinds of pepper to the food processor. Process until combined.

2   Heat the remaining 3 tablespoons of oil in a large, heavy-duty roasting pan set over medium heat. Sear the lamb on all sides until deeply browned, 3 to 4 minutes per side. (You'll need to prop up and support the leg with tongs to sear some areas.)

3   Set the leg in the pan with the flatter side down. Spread the bread crumb mixture evenly on top of the leg and partially down the sides. Roast until medium-rare, 70 to 80 minutes, when an instant-read thermometer inserted into the deepest section of meat (without touching the bone) reads 130°F. Let the meat rest for at least 20 minutes before carving.

Stilton-Stuffed Burgers

with Caramelized Red Onions and Balsamic Vinegar

SERVES 4

This twist on the revered hamburger is so successful that you may decide to skip the usual toasted bun and squirt of ketchup. Rather than melting a slice of cheese on top, like the classic cheeseburger, these burgers hide it in the center. If you like blue cheese, there's no greater treat than biting into a nugget of warm, runny blue cheese. Serve the red onions as a side dish or as a topping for the burger.

Ingredients

2 tablespoons extra-virgin olive oil, plus more as needed

1½ pounds red onions, thinly sliced (about 4 cups)

2 tablespoons balsamic vinegar

1 teaspoon coarse salt

⅛ teaspoon freshly ground black pepper

1½ pounds ground beef

3 ounces firm blue-veined cheese, such as Stilton, crumbled

1 tablespoon finely chopped fresh Italian parsley

1   Heat a medium skillet, preferably cast-iron, over medium heat. Add the oil and heat until hot enough to sizzle an onion ring. Add the onions, adjust the heat to medium-low, and sauté, stirring, for 2 minutes, or until evenly coated with the oil. Cover and cook for 3 minutes, or until wilted. Uncover and cook, stirring occasionally and adjusting the heat between medium and medium-low, for about 20 minutes, or until the onions are a dark golden brown. Remove the skillet from the heat. Transfer the onions to a large bowl. Add the vinegar, salt, and pepper to the onions and set aside. Rinse and dry the pan.

2   Divide the ground beef into eight 3-ounce portions, and shape each portion into a patty about 4 inches in diameter. Divide 2 ounces (about ½ cup crumbled) of the cheese evenly among 4 of the patties, sprinkling it on the surface and lightly pressing

it into the meat. Top with the remaining 4 patties, to make 4 cheese-stuffed burgers. Press around the edge of each burger to seal the top and bottom patties together, to prevent the cheese from oozing out during cooking. Brush both sides of the burgers lightly with olive oil.

3   Heat the skillet over medium heat until hot enough for a drop of water to sizzle on contact. Place the burgers in the pan, increase the heat to high, and cook, flipping them at the midpoint, for 4 minutes per side for medium-rare and 5 minutes per side for well done. Transfer the burgers to a platter.

4   Add the onions to the hot skillet and reheat briefly over low heat for about 1 minute, or until hot. Spoon the onions over the burgers. Sprinkle with the remaining 1 ounce of cheese and the parsley, and serve.

Oven-Braised Short Ribs
with Fennel

SERVES 4 TO 6

Buttery, tender short ribs make a great company meal. It's best to cook short ribs, and other slow-cooked rich meat dishes, one day ahead so the juices can chill and you can lift off the excess fat, which will solidify on the surface. The recipe serves six, but to add more servings, simply increase the number of short ribs and the size of the cooking vessel.

1   If you want to keep the short ribs together, tie each one tightly across the bone with cooking string. Combine 1 tablespoon salt and ½ teaspoon black pepper. Rub over all the surfaces of the short ribs.

2   Heat a large nonreactive Dutch oven or saucepan over medium heat. Add the olive oil. When hot, add the ribs, being careful not to crowd them or they won't brown properly. (If the ribs don't all fit in the Dutch oven, brown them in two batches, or use a heavy skillet to brown any remaining ribs at the same time.) Cook, adjusting the heat between medium and medium-high to maintain a steady sizzle without getting the pan too hot, turning with tongs as needed, for about 3 minutes per side, or until browned. As the ribs are browned, transfer them to a large bowl.

Ingredients

- 3½ to 4 pounds meaty bone-in short ribs
- Coarse salt and freshly ground black pepper
- 2 tablespoons extra-virgin olive oil
- 1 cup diced yellow onion
- ½ cup diced celery
- ½ cup diced carrot
- 2 cloves garlic, coarsely chopped
- 1 tablespoon fennel seeds
- 2 cups full-bodied red wine
- 2 bay leaves
- 1 (28-ounce) can Italian plum tomatoes with juices

3   When all the ribs are browned, spoon off all but 1 tablespoon of fat from the pot. Add the onion, celery, and carrot, and cook over medium-low heat, stirring, for about 8 minutes, or until golden. Meanwhile, crush the garlic and fennel seeds together with a large knife. Add to the vegetables and cook for about 30 seconds, or until tender.

4   If necessary, rearrange the oven racks to accommodate the large size of the pan. Preheat the oven to 325°F.

5   Add the wine and bay leaves to the Dutch oven and bring to a boil. Boil for 5 minutes, or until reduced by half. Stir in the tomatoes and again bring to a boil, breaking up the tomatoes with the side of a large metal spoon. Add the browned ribs and any juices that accumulated in the bowl. Turn the ribs to coat them evenly.

6   Cover and cook for 2 to 2½ hours, until the meat is pulling away from the bones.

7   Use a slotted spoon to lift the ribs from the pot to a platter. Discard any loose bones. Snip off the strings and discard.

8   Pour the remaining contents through a strainer set over a large bowl. Discard the bay leaves and then spoon the strained vegetables onto the ribs. Cover the platter with aluminum foil and keep warm in the turned-off oven.

9   Spoon off and discard the fat that comes to the top of the bowl and then pour the juices into a small saucepan. Alternatively, chill the strained juices for several hours or overnight and lift off the fat that solidifies on top. Refrigerate the ribs and vegetables, tightly covered, and then return to the saucepan with the defatted juices and slowly reheat over low heat.

10 Taste and adjust the seasoning with salt and pepper. Pour the juices over the short ribs and serve hot.

Pot Roast
with Braised Onions
and Pan-Browned Potatoes

SERVES 4

A thick-cut boneless chuck steak is the best choice here. It's ideal for when you want a pot roast but don't want to cook a big roast with lots of leftovers. Chuck is generally well marbled and will cook up soft and tender.

1   Heat a large saucepan or Dutch oven over medium heat and pour in 1 tablespoon of olive oil. Tilt the pan to coat. Sprinkle the meat well on both sides with salt and pepper. Add to the pan and cook, adjusting the heat between medium and medium-high as needed, for about 5 minutes per side, or until well browned. Use tongs and a wide spatula to transfer the roast to a plate.

2   Add the onion wedges to the pan and cook over medium to medium-high heat, stirring, for 10 minutes, or until well browned. Season with the fresh or dried oregano and some salt and pepper. Transfer to a large bowl.

3   Add the remaining 1 tablespoon of oil to the hot pan and place the potatoes, cut side down, in the pan. Cook, without turning, for 10 minutes, until well browned on the cut side. Transfer the potatoes to the bowl with the onions. Set aside.

4   Add the chopped onion, the carrot, and the celery to the hot pan along with a drizzle of oil if the pan is dry. Cook over medium heat, stirring, for 3 minutes, or until tender. Pour in the wine, bring to a boil, and stir. Scrape the brown bits from the bottom of the pan. Boil for 2 minutes, or until the wine is reduced by half. Add the beef broth and tomato paste and bring to a boil, stirring until blended.

5   Return the meat and any juices that have accumulated on the plate to the pan. Spoon the broth over the meat. Cover and cook over low heat for about 1 hour, or until the meat is tender.

6   Gently lift the meat from the pan and place on a plate. Puree the juices and solids from the pan to make a sauce. Add the puree to the reserved onions and potatoes, and stir to combine. Slide the meat and juices back into the pan. Spoon the vegetable mixture on top of the meat. Cover and cook over low heat for 10 to 15 minutes, until the potatoes and onions are tender. Season to taste with salt and pepper.

7   Transfer the meat to a cutting board and cut crosswise into thick slices. Arrange the slices on a warmed platter and top with the vegetables and sauce. Sprinkle with the fresh oregano.

Walnut Pesto-Stuffed
Pork Roast

SERVES 8

In summer, when big bunches of fresh basil are sold everywhere, take advantage of the bounty and make pesto. Classic pesto is typically made with basil, pine nuts, and Pecorino Romano cheese, but this adaptation is made with walnuts and Parmesan cheese and is slathered in the center and on top of the pork roast. Because the loin is lean, brining is recommended for 12 to 24 hours before roasting.

1   One day before roasting the pork, make the brine. In a large bowl, dissolve the salt in the hot water. Add the cold water and the ice cubes. Place the pork in a large, heavy-duty resealable plastic bag. Add the brine and seal the bag closed. Seal it in a second plastic bag for reinforcement. (Or use any large container and cover it tightly.) Place on a rimmed sheet pan and refrigerate for 12 to 24 hours. When ready to cook, drain the brining liquid and discard, then wipe the roast dry with paper towels. Let stand at room temperature for 30 minutes before roasting.

2   Meanwhile, make the pesto. In a blender or food processor, combine the basil, ½ cup of the oil, the walnuts, garlic, salt, and pepper, and process until finely chopped. With the motor running, slowly add the remaining ½ cup of olive oil and process until the paste is well blended. Do not overprocess the pesto. You should be able to see small pieces of basil

Brine and Pork

- ½ cup coarse salt
- 1 cup hot water
- 2 quarts very cold water
- 1 cup ice cubes
- 1 (3½- to 4-pound) boneless pork loin, untied

Walnut Pesto

- 3 cups packed fresh basil leaves
- 1 cup extra-virgin olive oil
- ½ cup chopped walnuts
- 2 cloves garlic, chopped
- 1 teaspoon coarse salt
- ½ teaspoon freshly ground black pepper
- ⅔ cup grated Parmigiano-Reggiano cheese

. . . .

throughout. Transfer the pesto to a small bowl and stir in the cheese.

3   Preheat the oven to 400°F. Have ready a large roasting pan with a rack. Cut 8 pieces of cooking string each about 18 inches long. Place the pork loin on a cutting board and make a slit along the side from the top to the bottom, cutting just deep enough so the loin opens up and lies flat like a book. Slather the cut surface with ½ cup of the pesto. Fold it over and tie firmly, but not too tightly, at 1-inch intervals with the lengths of string.

4   Place the tied loin on the rack in the roasting pan. Roast for 45 minutes. Remove the pan from the oven and slather about ¼ cup of the remaining pesto on top of the roast. Continue roasting for 30 minutes longer, or until an instant-read thermometer registers 135°F. Remove from the oven and let rest for 10 minutes. As the pork rests, the internal temperature will rise to 145°F, which is medium-rare.

5   Lift the roast from the rack to a cutting board. Snip off the strings. Cut the pork into ½-inch-thick slices. Arrange the slices, overlapping them, on a large platter. Drizzle any juices from the cutting board over the meat. Serve warm or at room temperature. Pass the remaining pesto at the table.

Baby Back Ribs
with Cannellini Beans

SERVES 4

These small, meaty pork ribs are *slowly* cooked in a tomato-based sauce. Although paprika is not typical, it adds a pleasant depth of flavor to the rich sauce. Try smoked paprika for even more flavor. Once the ribs are tender, mix in the cooked cannellini beans and allow them to simmer long enough to absorb the flavors of the sauce.

1   With a sharp knife, cut through the meaty portion between the ribs to separate them. There should be about 12 ribs. Place the ribs in a large bowl, add 3 tablespoons salt and cold water to cover, and stir to combine. Let stand for 30 minutes. Drain off the brining liquid, rinse with cold water, drain again, and pat dry. Sprinkle lightly with additional salt and pepper.

2   Heat a large saucepan or Dutch oven over medium-high heat until hot enough for a drop of water to sizzle on contact. Add 1 tablespoon of the olive oil and half of the ribs. Cook the ribs, turning as needed and adjusting the heat as necessary to maintain a steady sizzle, for about 10 minutes, or until evenly browned. Transfer the ribs to a plate. Repeat with the remaining oil and ribs.

3   Discard all but 1 tablespoon of the fat. Add the onion and green pepper and cook over medium-low heat, stirring, for about 10 minutes, or until golden. Add the garlic and cook for 1 minute.

1 (2½-pound) rack baby back pork ribs

Coarse salt and freshly ground black pepper

2 tablespoons extra-virgin olive oil

1 cup chopped yellow onion

½ cup chopped green bell pepper

1 clove garlic, chopped

1½ teaspoons sweet or smoked paprika

2 cups crushed tomatoes

1 cup low-sodium chicken broth or water

1 cinnamon stick

¼ teaspoon crushed red pepper

1 (2 by ½-inch) strip orange zest

2 (15-ounce) cans cannellini beans, rinsed and drained

2 tablespoons finely chopped fresh Italian parsley

....

Stir in the paprika until blended. Add the tomatoes and broth and bring to a boil. Add the cinnamon, red pepper, and orange zest, and stir to mix. Decrease the heat to low and cook, uncovered, for 5 minutes.

4   Transfer the ribs and any juices that have accumulated on the plate into the saucepan. Spoon the sauce over the ribs and cover. Cook over medium-low to low heat for 1 hour, or until the meat is pulling away from the bones. Taste the sauce and adjust the seasoning with salt and pepper.

5   Add the beans and stir well to combine. Cook, covered, over low heat for 25 minutes, or until the beans have taken on the flavors of the sauce.

6   Sprinkle the parsley over the ribs. Spoon the ribs, beans, and sauce into warmed shallow bowls and serve at once.

Chard, Mushroom, and Swiss Cheese Frittata

SERVES 6

Eggs are a comforting dish any time of the day. The secret ingredient here is Dijon mustard. You won't taste it, but it's working behind the scenes to deepen the flavor.

1   Preheat the oven to 350°F.

2   Trim the stems from the chard leaves. Discard the stems. Immerse the leaves in water to rid them of grit. Lift them out and drain. Chop the leaves coarsely.

3   Heat 3 tablespoons of the oil in a 10-inch ovenproof skillet over medium-high heat. Add the mushrooms, sprinkle lightly with salt, and sauté, stirring frequently, until golden brown, 5 to 7 minutes. Lower the heat to medium, add the shallots, and cook until the shallots are softened but not browned, about 30 seconds. Add the chard a few handfuls at a time and cook, tossing until soft and wilted, about 4 minutes. Add ¼ teaspoon of salt and continue cooking and tossing until all the liquid in the pan evaporates, about 3 more minutes. Turn off the heat.

4   Whisk the eggs, half-and-half, mustard, the remaining ½ teaspoon salt, and several grinds of pepper together in a medium bowl. Stir in the cheese. Add the remaining 1 tablespoon olive oil to the skillet and heat over medium heat.

Ingredients

1 pound Swiss chard

¼ cup extra-virgin olive oil

8 ounces white mushrooms, thinly sliced

¾ teaspoon kosher salt, plus more for sprinkling

¼ cup minced shallots

8 large eggs

¼ cup half-and-half

1 teaspoon Dijon mustard

Freshly ground black pepper

1⅔ cups (5 ounces) grated Gruyère or Jarlsberg cheese

Spread out the vegetables evenly and, when the pan is hot, pour in the egg mixture. Cook until the bottom is set, about 3 minutes, and then transfer the skillet to the oven. Bake until the eggs are set on top, about 15 minutes.

5   Place the frittata under the broiler a few inches from the heat source until the top is golden, 2 to 3 minutes. Remove from the heat and let rest for a few minutes; the frittata will pull away from the sides of the pan. Slice in the pan or else flip the frittata onto a plate and serve.

Savory Meat Loaf with Maple-Mustard Glaze
and Rich Brown Gravy

SERVES 6

This version is what all those stodgy meat loaves of your childhood should have been: juicy, tender, and savory. The mixture of meats makes the flavor complex, but take care as you work them together—you want them well blended but you don't want to compact them as you go, which would make the meat loaf dense and heavy. The gravy may be gilding the lily, but why not? Its glossy mahogany color and rich flavor are perfect with a scoop of mashed potatoes.

1   Heat the oil in a medium skillet over medium heat, add the onion and ½ teaspoon salt, and sauté, stirring frequently until the onion is deep golden, very soft, and fragrant, 15 to 20 minutes. Add the garlic and continue cooking until the garlic is soft and fragrant, too, another 2 to 3 minutes; don't let the garlic burn. Cool the onion mixture.

2   Preheat the oven to 350°F. Pour the milk over the bread crumbs in a bowl and let them absorb the milk for at least 10 minutes. Chop the bacon finely (partially freezing it will make this easier; or cut into 1-inch pieces and then chop in a food processor).

3   In a large bowl, whisk together the egg, green chiles, ketchup, 1 tablespoon of mustard, 2 teaspoons of Worcestershire sauce, 1 teaspoon salt, the black pepper, and the hot sauce. Gently crumble the beef, pork, and sausage into the bowl, mixing as you add them. Add the chopped bacon and the soaked bread crumbs. Very gently but thoroughly mix everything together with your clean hands. The goal is to distribute the meats and seasonings so that they're all blended without squeezing or compacting the mixture too much.

4   Test for seasoning by frying a spoonful of the meat mixture and then tasting it. Add more salt, pepper, or hot sauce as needed.

5   If not making the gravy, use a rimmed baking sheet or Pyrex baking dish lined with parchment (the meat loaves will render a lot of fat and liquid, so this makes cleanup easier). If making gravy, use a small roasting pan or large ovenproof skillet and no parchment, as you will be putting this pan on the stovetop later. Divide the raw meat loaf in two and pat each half into a 6 by 4-inch loaf, about 3 inches high. Arrange the loaves side by side on the baking sheet or roasting pan and bake for about 20 minutes.

6   To make the glaze, whisk together the remaining 1 tablespoon mustard, the remaining 1 teaspoon Worcestershire, and the maple syrup and brush this glaze over the meat loaves. Continue baking until completely cooked. An instant-read thermometer should register 160°F (the temperature will continue to rise a bit). Transfer the meat loaves to a cutting board or tray to rest about 15 minutes before slicing and serving.

7   To make the gravy, pour off all but about 1 tablespoon of fat from the pan, taking care to keep the meat juices and browned bits in the pan. Put the pan over medium heat, add the flour, and scrape with a wooden spoon or a flat whisk to blend the flour as well as scrape up the browned bits. Cook for about 1 minute. Whisk in the broth and any juices that have accumulated around the resting meat loaves. Simmer until slightly reduced and thick but not gloppy. Taste and adjust the seasoning with salt and pepper. Serve hot.

Old-Fashioned Tomato and Meat Sauce for Pasta

SERVES 6

This rich tomato sauce is excellent served with rigatoni or other sturdy dried pasta with ridges that will hold the sauce. The meat in this recipe—pork ribs and beef chuck—adds to the rich flavor. However, meatballs, Italian sausage, veal stew meat, Italian fennel sausage, or even a browned pork chop or piece of beef sirloin can be substituted. Just make sure not to use more than 3 pounds of meat, which is served on the side with the pasta.

1   Blot the meat dry with paper towels, and sprinkle generously on all sides with salt and pepper. Heat the oil in a large wide pan over medium heat. Working in batches, add the meat to the oil and cook, turning with tongs, for 10 to 15 minutes, until browned on all sides. As each batch is done, transfer it to a large plate.

2   Spoon off all but about 2 tablespoons of fat in the pan. Add the onion and cook over medium heat, stirring, for 5 minutes, or until golden. Add the garlic and cook for 1 minute, or until softened. Remove from the heat.

3   Puree the tomatoes in a food processor. Add the pureed tomatoes, tomato sauce, tomato paste, oregano, and red pepper to the pan and stir to blend.

Ingredients

1 to 1½ pounds meaty pork spareribs or country-style ribs

1 to 1½ pounds boneless beef chuck or stew meat, cut into 2-inch pieces

Coarse salt and freshly ground black pepper

2 tablespoons extra-virgin olive oil

½ cup coarsely chopped onion

3 cloves garlic, minced

3 (28-ounce) cans Italian plum tomatoes with juices

1 (16-ounce) can tomato sauce

1 (6-ounce) can tomato paste

1 teaspoon dried oregano

Pinch of crushed red pepper (optional)

1 pound rigatoni, penne rigate, or conchiglie (large shells)

Grated Parmigiano-Reggiano or Pecorino Romano cheese, for serving

4 Add the browned meats and any juices that accumulated on the plate to the pan and turn the heat to medium-low. Cook, uncovered, stirring and adjusting the temperature to maintain a slow simmer, for 2 to 2½ hours, until the sauce is thickened and slightly reduced.

5 Fill a deep pot three-quarters full with water. Bring the water to a rolling boil. Add 3 tablespoons of coarse salt to the boiling water and then gradually add the pasta. Stir until the water returns to a boil. Boil the pasta for 10 minutes. Remove a piece of pasta with the slotted spoon and test for doneness. Pasta is cooked when it is only slightly resistant to the bite. If the pasta is too hard, cook for 2 minutes more and test again. Keep testing the pasta every 2 minutes, or until it is cooked to your liking.

6 Set a large colander in the sink and pour the pasta and water slowly into the colander. Do not shake all of the water off the pasta.

7 Ladle a pool of just the sauce—no meat—in the bottom of a large serving bowl. Add half of the pasta. Top with another ladle or two of sauce, again without the meat. Top with the remaining pasta. Top with 2 more ladles of the sauce. Gently mix the pasta with the sauce until evenly coated. Reserve the remaining sauce.

8 Lift the meat from the sauce and either arrange it along the edges of the pasta or place it in a separate serving bowl. Pour the remaining tomato sauce into a gravy boat or a small bowl, and serve along with the pasta and meat. Pass the cheese at the table.

Crispy Fried Chicken
with Indulgent Gravy

Ingredients

2 pounds skin-on, bone-in chicken pieces (thighs and legs will stay juicier than breasts)

2 cups buttermilk

Coarse salt

½ teaspoon hot sauce, such as Tabasco

1 cup unbleached all-purpose flour

½ teaspoon freshly ground black pepper

Canola, peanut, or grapeseed oil, for frying

Gravy

1 tablespoon all-purpose flour

1 cup low-sodium or homemade chicken broth

½ cup whole milk

¼ cup heavy cream or crème fraîche

Fresh lemon juice, to taste

SERVES 4 TO 6

Some contemporary cooks are wary of frying, but here's a reason to make an exception. This chicken is so moist, so crunchy and savory, it's worth any trepidation. The key is to use a pan that doesn't crowd the chicken (use two, or cook in batches, if necessary), and—most importantly—to keep an eye on the heat. The chicken should sizzle merrily in the oil but it shouldn't brown too quickly or the outside will be done before the inside is fully cooked.

1   Arrange the chicken in a baking dish or tray. Whisk the buttermilk, 1 teaspoon salt, and the hot sauce together and pour over the chicken. Cover, refrigerate, and marinate for at least 3 hours or up to 8 hours.

2   When you're ready to fry, whisk together the flour, 1 tablespoon salt, and the black pepper and pile onto a large plate or tray. Arrange the chicken and the flour next to the stovetop.

3   Add about ½ inch oil to a large heavy skillet at least 12 inches in diameter. If your pan is smaller, use two pans or fry the chicken in batches. Heat the oil over medium-high heat to about 375°F. (If you don't have a thermometer, drop a 1-inch piece of bread into the oil. It should take about 60 seconds to become deep golden brown.)

4   Pick up a piece of chicken, let the buttermilk drip off, then dredge the piece through the seasoned flour, making sure all the creases and corners are well coated. Add each piece to the hot oil carefully, skin side down. Continue with all the chicken, keeping an eye on the temperature. You want the oil to sizzle in a lively fashion, but you don't want the chicken browning too quickly.

5   Once all the chicken is in the pan, turn the heat to medium so the sizzling is steady but not too wild and then cover the pan. After about 15 minutes, remove the lid and check the chicken. If a rich brown crust has developed, turn each piece. If the chicken still looks pale, increase the heat a tiny bit and cook for a few more minutes before turning. Continue frying the chicken until well browned on the second side and the meat is totally tender when pierced with a knife, 30 to 40 minutes total. Don't let the browned bits in the bottom of the pan burn.

6   Remove the pan from the heat and transfer the chicken to a rack.

7   To make the gravy, skim off all the fat from the skillet except about a tablespoon, capturing any crisp bits in the skimmer and reserving them. Put the pan back over medium-high heat, add the flour, and with a flat whisk blend with the fat. Add the broth and whisk until the browned bits in the pan are dissolved. Simmer until reduced by about half, 3 to 4 minutes, whisking frequently. Add the milk and cream, and continue simmering until slightly reduced, creamy, and the flavor is deep and mellow. Add back any reserved crisp bits, squeeze in a few drops of lemon juice to taste, and adjust the salt and pepper. Serve in a gravy pitcher with the chicken pieces.

Corn Tortillas Casserole

SERVES 6

Known as a *sopa seca*, or "dry soup," this casserole is the definition of Mexican comfort food. Corn tortillas cut into strips are layered with spicy tomato sauce, roasted poblano chiles, and two types of cheese, one soft and melting and the other dry and sharp. The top is spiced with sour cream or Mexican *crema*, a rich, thick cream available in Mexican grocers, and then the whole thing is baked.

1   Heat a large sauté pan or skillet over medium heat. Add the oil and onion to the pan and cook, stirring, for about 3 minutes, or until softened. Add the garlic and cook for 1 minute, or until fragrant. Add the tomato puree, chile and adobo sauce, and salt, and bring to a gentle boil, stirring. Decrease the heat to low and cook, uncovered, for 10 minutes, or until thickened.

2   Preheat the broiler. Char the skin of the poblano, turning with tongs, for 10 to 15 minutes, until evenly blackened and blistered. Place the charred poblano in a bowl, cover with aluminum foil or plastic wrap, and let stand for about 20 minutes, or until cool enough to handle and the skin has loosened. Rub the charred skin off the cooled chile with your fingertips, or use the tip of a small knife. Rinse with water, then slit the chile along its length and open it flat. Cut out and discard the stem, and scrape away the seeds and white membranes with the tip of a spoon. Cut the poblano lengthwise into ¼-inch-wide strips and set aside.

3   Line a tray with paper towels. Pour oil to a depth of ½ inch into a 10-inch skillet, place over medium heat, and heat until a tortilla strip dropped into the oil sizzles on contact. Working in small batches, fry the tortilla strips for 10 to 20 seconds, until they begin to crisp but not brown. Use a slotted spoon or skimmer to transfer the tortilla strips to the prepared tray. Repeat until all the tortilla strips are fried.

4   Preheat the oven to 350°F. Spread one-third of the sauce in a 10 by 2-inch round or a 10½ by 8½ by 2-inch baking dish. Layer half of the tortilla strips on top. Sprinkle with one-third each *queso Chihuahua* and *queso añejo*. Layer half of the poblano strips on top.

Spread with half of the remaining tomato sauce and layer with all of the remaining tortilla strips, half of each cheese, and all of the remaining poblano strips. Add a final layer of tomato sauce and then a layer of both cheeses. Spread the sour cream over the top.

5   Bake for 35 to 40 minutes, until the casserole is hot and bubbly. Let stand for 10 minutes and serve.

Luxuriously Retro Beef Stroganoff

with Buttered Noodles

SERVES 6

"Retro" and "elegant" don't often go together, but this dish is the epitome of both, conjuring up swank dinner parties of the 1960s and '70s. And there's a reason it's been such a hit through the years: It's delicious. For entertaining, make the dish ahead and gently reheat it—don't let the sauce boil or the sour cream may curdle. Wide egg noodles are the traditional accompaniment, but some creamy polenta would be delicious, too, and a touch more nutritious.

1   Cut about half the mushrooms into ⅛-inch slices and the other half into quarters. Heat 1 tablespoon of the oil in a large skillet over medium-high heat. Add all the sliced mushrooms, season lightly with salt and pepper, and cook, stirring frequently, until the mushrooms are lightly browned and most of the moisture has been cooked off, 7 to 9 minutes. Transfer to a bowl. Repeat with another tablespoon of oil and the quartered mushrooms, and transfer them to the same bowl.

2   Return the pan to the heat. Add another tablespoon oil and the onions. Reduce the heat to medium-low, season lightly with salt, and cook until soft, fragrant, and translucent but

not browned, about 7 minutes. Transfer to the bowl with the mushrooms.

3   Toss the beef with the flour in a bowl and season with salt and pepper. Add another tablespoon oil to the pan, heat over medium-high heat, add about half the beef, and cook very quickly until lightly browned but still quite rare, about 1 minute. Transfer to the bowl with the mushrooms. Repeat with the rest of the beef (or cook all the beef at once in 2 large pans).

4   Put the pan back on medium heat, add the tomato paste, and cook, scraping up all the browned bits in the pan, about 1 minute. Add the broth, adjust the heat so that the broth reaches a moderate boil, and cook until the broth has reduced to about 3 cups. Whisk in the Dijon, Worcestershire, and thyme, then whisk in the sour cream. Turn down the heat to avoid an actual boil (which could cause the sour cream to curdle), and then simmer for a few minutes to let the sauce thicken a bit. Taste and adjust seasonings with more salt, black pepper, Worcestershire, or mustard.

5   Add the mushrooms, onion, and beef to the sauce. Keep warm, but not over too high heat (which could cause the sauce to separate).

6   Meanwhile, bring a large pot of water to a boil, salt it generously, and boil the noodles according to the package instructions. Drain well, toss with the butter, divide among 6 bowls, and ladle over a generous portion of the stroganoff. Sprinkle with herbs, if using, and serve.

Arroz con Pollo

with Chorizo and Capers

SERVES 6

When using a cut-up chicken (rather than only legs and thighs), take precautions to keep the breast meat from drying out. The trick is to sear the breast pieces briefly and then add them to the rice halfway through cooking. Mexican chorizo, a fresh sausage seasoned with garlic and paprika, delivers more authentic flavor. Look for it in Hispanic groceries.

1   Cut the chorizo in half lengthwise, then crosswise into 1-inch chunks. (It's easier if the casing side is up; the casing shouldn't come off, but if it does, just discard it.)

2   Pat the chicken pieces dry with paper towels. Season with 2 teaspoons salt and a few grinds of pepper. Heat the oil in a medium (5-quart) Dutch oven or heavy casserole over medium-high heat. Sear the drumsticks and thighs until deeply golden on all sides, 7 to 10 minutes (use a splatter screen if you have one). Transfer the pieces to a large bowl. Sear the breast pieces on the skin side only until golden. Transfer them to the bowl. Lower the heat to medium and sear the chorizo, stirring frequently, until golden brown, 2 to 3 minutes. Transfer the chorizo to the bowl.

3   Pour off and discard all but 1 tablespoon of oil. Spoon out any burnt bits. Combine the cumin, paprika, turmeric, and chili

powder in a small dish. Set the pot back over medium heat and add the onion and bell pepper. Cook for 2 minutes, stirring often; the moisture in the vegetables will deglaze the browned drippings in the pan. Add the garlic and cook, stirring, for 1 minute to let the flavors bloom.

4   Add the wine, tomatoes, the remaining ½ teaspoon salt, and the bay leaf. Increase the heat to medium-high and simmer for 2 minutes. Add the chicken and chorizo to the pot. Add the rice and broth. Bring to a boil, cover, lower the heat to medium-low, and simmer for 9 minutes.

5   Remove the pan from the heat and let rest, covered, for 5 minutes. Sprinkle the capers on top of the rice. When spooning out portions, look for the bay leaf and discard it. Serve with the lemon wedges and hot sauce.

Side Dishes

SIDE
DISHES

Roasted Garlic
Mashed Potatoes

SERVES 4

Roasted garlic adds deep flavor to the russet potato, also known as the baking or Idaho potato. This type has low moisture and high starch, qualities that yield wonderfully light, buttery mashed potatoes. Use the leftover roasted garlic paste on sandwiches, in vinaigrettes, rubbed under the skin of chicken breasts, or swirled into a bowl of steaming soup. To store it, cover with a thin layer of olive oil, cap tightly, and refrigerate. It will keep for several weeks.

1   Preheat the oven to 350°F.

2   Rub the outside of each garlic head on its side and cut ½ inch off the top. Place the heads, cut side up, in a garlic roaster or small baking dish. Drizzle each head with 1 tablespoon of olive oil. Cover with a lid or aluminum foil. Or dispense with the dish and wrap each garlic head in a piece of heavy-duty aluminum foil. Roast for 1 hour, or until the cloves are soft. Remove from the oven and let cool.

3   Separate the cloves of garlic. Have ready a small bowl. One at a time, pinch each clove at the stem end and then press on the clove to squeeze the softened garlic out into the bowl. Add a pinch of salt and a grinding of pepper and mash with a fork until blended.

4   In a large pot, combine the potatoes and bay leaves and add water to cover. Bring to a boil over high heat and add 1 tablespoon of salt. Lower the heat to medium, cover partially, and cook for 15 to 20 minutes, until the potatoes are tender when pierced with a fork. Drain in a colander and discard the bay leaf.

5   Return the potatoes to the pot and mash with a potato masher.

6   Add half the roasted garlic and ¼ cup of the olive oil and beat with a wooden spoon until blended. Season to taste with salt and pepper. If you want a more pronounced garlic flavor, add the remaining mashed garlic.

7   Mound the potatoes in a warmed serving bowl. Pass the olive oil at the table for guests to add to taste.

Apple and Ginger Spiced
Sweet Potatoes

Ingredients

2 pounds sweet potatoes

Coarse salt and freshly ground
   black pepper

1 cup unsweetened apple juice

2 tablespoons unsalted butter

1 teaspoon peeled grated fresh
   ginger

1 tablespoon minced fresh chives
   or thinly sliced green onion
   tops, for garnish

SERVES 4

The potatoes for this simple mashed sweet potato dish can be boiled or baked. Cook them whole in their skins, then peel them and pass the soft flesh through a potato ricer, food mill, or even an old-fashioned potato masher. Any color sweet potato or any mix of colors can be used, such as orange-fleshed Red Garnets or Jewels and cream-colored Hannahs. A splash of apple juice and a bit of finely grated ginger add a fresh spark to this old favorite.

1   Place the sweet potatoes in a large saucepan and add water to cover. Bring to a boil over high heat, cover partially, reduce the heat to medium-low, and cook for 30 minutes, or until tender when pierced with a skewer. Drain in a colander and let cool. Use a paring knife to pull off the skins. Cut the potatoes into 1-inch chunks and puree. Season the potatoes with salt and a grinding of pepper.

2   Rinse and dry the saucepan. Add the apple juice, butter, and ginger, place over low heat, and warm, stirring with a wooden spoon, until the butter is melted. Remove from the heat.

3   Add the potatoes to the saucepan. Reheat over low heat, stirring with a wooden spoon, until hot. Spoon into a warmed serving dish and garnish with the chives.

Yukon Gold and Sweet Potato Gratin

with Three Cheeses

SERVES 6 TO 8

Potato gratins are classic, but the combination of yellow Yukon Gold potatoes and orange sweet potatoes is novel. Rosemary gives the creamy sauce a distinctive profile that goes well with big flavors like grilled salmon, steaks, or lamb chops.

1   In a large heavy pan, combine the milk, cream, salt, rosemary, garlic, and pepper. Place over medium heat and heat, stirring, for 3 minutes, or until small bubbles appear around the edges of the pan. Add the Yukon Gold and sweet potatoes, stir to coat, and simmer gently, uncovered, for 10 to 12 minutes, until the potatoes are partially cooked. Remove from the heat.

2   Preheat the oven to 400°F. Rub the butter over the bottom and sides of a 2-quart gratin dish.

3   Use a slotted spoon to transfer half the potatoes to the gratin dish. Sprinkle with half each of the Gruyère, Cheddar, and Parmigiano-Reggiano cheeses. Add the remaining potatoes. Use two forks to arrange the top layer of potatoes in a slightly overlapping design, evenly distributing the different-colored

potatoes. Ladle the hot cream mixture over the potatoes and sprinkle with all of the remaining cheeses.

4   Bake for 35 minutes, or until the potatoes are tender when pierced with a skewer or the tip of a knife and the gratin is bubbling and golden.

5   Let the gratin rest for 10 minutes before serving.

Crispy Roasted Potato Wedges

with Parsley, Rosemary, and Lemon

SERVES 4 TO 6

With a little chopping of herbs and garlic, you can amp up your everyday roasted potatoes to something special. Lemon zest and parsley add sparkle, and the generous coating of olive oil helps ensure crispness.

1   Preheat the oven to 450°F. Finely chop the garlic and put it in a large bowl. Add the oil, parsley, and rosemary.

2   Cut the potatoes into ¾- to 1-inch-wide wedges. Add to the bowl and sprinkle with the salt. Toss with your hands to coat the potatoes evenly with the herbed oil.

3   Spread the potatoes on a large rimmed baking sheet, scraping the bowl of any extra oil and herbs, and arrange them with a flat side down. Roast until the bottoms of the potatoes turn golden, about 25 minutes, then turn them with a metal spatula (some potatoes will stick, so do your best to scrape them loose). Continue roasting until golden and crisp outside and tender inside, about 15 minutes more. Gently sprinkle with the lemon zest.

4 Transfer the potatoes to a serving bowl, making sure to scrape up all the herbs and zest. Add several squeezes of lemon juice over the top. Toss gently to distribute. Serve hot.

Creamy Polenta
with Two Cheeses

SERVES 4 TO 6

Stirring polenta over low heat until the texture is soft and the flavor is sweet requires time, patience, and fortitude. Here, the double boiler comes to the rescue. Cook and stir the polenta in the top part over direct heat for a short period and then place it over simmering water in the bottom portion. The polenta will cook slowly without needing stirring and will emerge soft and fluffy 45 labor-free minutes later.

1   Heat the butter in the top of a large double boiler over low heat until melted. Stir in the onion and cook, stirring, for 5 minutes, or until softened. Add 2 cups of the water and bring to a boil.

2   In a bowl, stir together the cornmeal, the remaining 2 cups of water, and the salt until blended. Slowly whisk the wet cornmeal mixture into the boiling liquid until blended. Cook over low heat, stirring constantly, for 5 minutes, until the polenta begins to thicken.

3   Add water to a depth of 2 inches to the bottom of the double boiler and bring to a simmer over medium heat. Place the top of the double boiler with the precooked polenta over the simmering water. Make sure the bottom of the top part is not touching the water. Decrease the heat to medium-low, cover, and cook the polenta for 45 minutes, or until thick and fluffy.

Stir in the Parmigiano-Reggiano and mozzarella until melted. Taste and adjust the seasoning with salt.

4   Serve at once or keep warm over hot water until ready to serve, up to 1 hour. If the polenta gets too thick, stir in a small amount of water, broth, or milk to thin to the desired consistency.

Classic Extra-Cheesy Macaroni and Cheese

with Crunchy Crumb Topping

SERVES 4 TO 6

Hurray for real mac and cheese. It's crazy to eat the stuff from the box when the real deal is so easy to make and so totally superior. Do use a cheese with some character, however, or the bland noodles will dominate.

1   Preheat the oven to 375°F. Melt 3 tablespoons of the butter in a medium, heavy-based saucepan over medium heat. Add the flour and whisk until smooth; cook 2 to 3 minutes, whisking frequently. Slowly pour in the milk, whisking vigorously. If the sauce gets lumpy, don't worry; just keep whisking until smooth. Lower the heat and simmer for 7 to 8 minutes, whisking frequently, until creamy and smooth. Add 1½ teaspoons salt, the mustard and nutmeg if using, and the black pepper.

2   Take the pan off the heat and add 2½ cups of the Cheddar and half the Parmesan cheese. Whisk until the cheese is melted and the sauce is smooth. Taste and add more seasonings if you like. It should be salted well, as the sauce will flavor the macaroni.

3   Meanwhile, bring a large pot of water to a boil, add 2 tablespoons salt, and boil the macaroni according to the package directions. Drain well, return to the pot, then toss with the sauce until thoroughly coated. Pile into a 13 by 9-inch baking dish or four 6-inch cast-iron skillets. Sprinkle evenly with the remaining Cheddar and Parmesan.

4   Melt the remaining 2 tablespoons butter and toss with the bread crumbs; distribute over the macaroni. Bake until the topping is browned and the macaroni is hot, about 20 minutes. Let rest for about 10 minutes before serving.

Variations: While the classic is always welcome, try mixing things up on occasion by adding zippy green chiles or briny tuna. For a smoky green chile version, add 1 drained 4-ounce can diced mild green chiles before you put the macaroni in the baking dish. Mix 1 teaspoon smoked paprika with the crumbs and butter.

For the "tuna melt" version, substitute 1 cup grated Havarti or Fontina cheese for 1 cup of the Cheddar when you make the sauce (you'll still need a total of 3 cups cheese plus the ½ cup Parmesan). Add 2 drained 5-ounce cans tuna and 2 teaspoons grated lemon zest to the macaroni before you put it in the baking dish.

Desserts

Classic Crosshatch
Peanut Butter Cookies

MAKES ABOUT 50 COOKIES

Whether you like your peanut butter cookies made with chunky peanut butter or smooth, these classic cookies are rich and crumbly, perfect with a glass of milk. The peanut is actually a legume that grows underground. It made its debut at the St. Louis World's Fair in 1904 and has remained a beloved American food since then.

Ingredients

½ cup (1 stick) unsalted butter, softened

½ cup tightly packed light brown sugar

½ cup granulated sugar

1 large egg, at room temperature

1 teaspoon pure vanilla extract

¾ cup creamy or chunky peanut butter, at room temperature

1¾ cups unbleached all-purpose flour

½ teaspoon baking soda

¼ teaspoon salt

1   Position an oven rack in the top third of the oven and preheat the oven to 350°F. Line two baking sheets with parchment paper.

2   Put the butter, the brown sugar, and the ½ cup granulated sugar in a large bowl. Using a mixer, beat on low speed for 1 minute. Turn up the speed to medium and beat for another minute. The mixture should be blended and smooth. Scrape down the sides of the bowl. Add the egg and vanilla and beat on low speed until well blended. Add the peanut butter and beat until well blended. Scrape down the sides of the bowl.

3   Put the flour, baking soda, and salt in a medium bowl and whisk until blended. Add the dry ingredients to the batter and beat on low speed just until the dough is smooth and no patches of flour are visible. Scrape down the bowl one last time, and make sure no clumps of flour are hiding in the bottom.

4 Use an ice-cream scoop to shape the dough into cookies. You can also shape the dough by measuring out 1 level tablespoon for each cookie, and then rolling the dough between your palms into a ball. Space the balls about 2 inches apart on the prepared baking sheets.

5 Use a fork to press down firmly on top of each ball once in each direction, to form a crisscross pattern.

6 Place one baking sheet on each oven rack. Bake for 5 minutes, then switch the pans between the oven racks. Bake for another 6 to 7 minutes, until the cookies are golden brown around the edges. Transfer the pans to the cooling racks and let the cookies cool completely. You may need to reuse the pans to finish baking all the cookies. Let the pans cool before you put more dough on them for baking. Store the cookies in an airtight container or a resealable plastic bag for 5 days.

Mile-High
Apple Pie

SERVES 8

The attractive high dome of an apple pie can be considered a ruse, as the apples have shrunk, leaving a big space between the filling and the crust. Precooking the apples will minimize the gap and concentrate the apple flavor, too. Cream cheese pie dough makes assembling the pastry a breeze.

1   To make the dough, put the flour and salt in a food processor and pulse briefly to combine them. Scatter the butter and cream cheese over the top and pulse about 12 times, or just until the dough begins to clump together (butter pieces will still be visible). Turn the dough out onto a lightly floured work surface and gather it together.

2   Divide the dough in half, and shape each half into a disk. Wrap each disk in plastic wrap. Refrigerate until chilled but not hard, 1 to 2 hours.

3   To make the filling, peel and quarter the apples, and cut out the core from each quarter. Cut each quarter lengthwise into thirds and place in a large bowl. As you add the slices to the bowl, occasionally sprinkle and toss the apples with lemon juice. (Don't wait until all the apples are cut, or the first slices will have already turned brown.)

. . . .
Ingredients

Pie Dough

2 cups unbleached all-purpose flour

¼ teaspoon salt

10 tablespoons (1¼ sticks) cold unsalted butter, cut into tablespoons

6 ounces cream cheese (not low-fat), at room temperature, cut into ¾-inch pieces

Filling

4 pounds Golden Delicious apples

2 tablespoons fresh lemon juice

4 tablespoons (½ stick) unsalted butter

½ cup plus 1 teaspoon sugar

3 tablespoons unbleached all-purpose flour

¾ teaspoon ground cinnamon

1 tablespoon heavy cream or whole milk

. . . .

4 In a large skillet, melt 2 tablespoons of the butter over medium-high heat. Add half the apples and ¼ cup of the sugar. Cook, stirring often, for about 7 minutes, or until the apples are barely tender when pierced with the tip of a sharp knife. Transfer to a large bowl or rimmed baking sheet. Repeat with the remaining 2 tablespoons butter, the second half of the apples, and another ¼ cup sugar. If your skillet is smaller than 12 inches, cook the apples in three batches. Let the filling cool completely, stirring occasionally. Sprinkle the flour and cinnamon over the cooled filling and toss well.

5 Position a rack in the center of the oven, and place a rimmed baking sheet on the rack. Preheat the oven to 375°F.

6 Lightly flour a work surface, and draw a 12-inch circle in the flour. This guide will be the perfect size for a standard 9-inch pie dish. Place 1 dough disk in the center of the circle, and dust a little flour on top. Using the circle as a guide, roll out the dough into a 12-inch round about ⅛ inch thick. Loosely roll the dough around the rolling pin, center the pin over the pie dish, and carefully unroll the round over a 9-inch pie dish, easing it into the bottom and sides and allowing the excess to overhang the sides. Fill with the apples. Trim the overhanging dough to ½ inch. Roll out the remaining pie dough into a second 12-inch round. Transfer the dough round

the same way, centering it over the apple filling. Fold the overhang of the upper round under the edge of the bottom crust. Pinch the crusts together and flute the edge attractively. Cut a small hole in the center of the pie to allow steam to escape. Freeze for 15 minutes or refrigerate for 30 minutes.

7 Lightly brush the top crust with the cream. Sprinkle the top crust with the remaining teaspoon of sugar.

8 Place the pie on the hot baking sheet and bake for 40 to 50 minutes, until the top is golden brown. Let cool on a wire rack for at least 1 hour. Serve warm or at room temperature.

Apricot-Cherry Almond Cobbler

SERVES 6 TO 8

Apricots, cherries, and almonds are all members of the same botanical family, *Prunus*, which accounts for the natural way their flavors support and enhance each other. There is a double dose of almond here to accent the fruit filling within. The cakelike topping bursts with the rich presence of almond paste, while almond liqueur gives a hint of flavor when tossed with the sliced fruit.

1   Preheat the oven to 350°F and position an oven rack in the center.

2   Toss together the apricot slices, cherries, ½ cup sugar, and amaretto in a large bowl until all the fruit is coated evenly. Scrape into a baking dish and spread in an even layer.

3   Place the remaining ¼ cup sugar and almond paste in the bowl of a stand mixer and beat on medium speed until the almond paste is broken into tiny pieces. Add the butter and beat on medium-high until the mixture is light in color, almost white, 4 to 5 minutes. Scrape down the bowl. Add the egg and vanilla and blend well. Scrape down the bowl. In a medium bowl, whisk together the flour, baking powder, and salt. With the mixer on the lowest speed, add the dry ingredients and milk alternately to the butter. Scrape down the bowl and finish blending by hand. To cover the fruit, let the batter fall off a

. . . .
Ingredients

1 pound firm but ripe tart apricots, halved, pitted, and each half cut into 4 or 5 slices

1 pound firm but ripe cherries, pitted

¾ cup sugar

1 teaspoon amaretto (almond liqueur)

2½ ounces almond paste, at room temperature

6 tablespoons (¾ stick) unsalted butter, softened

1 large egg, at room temperature

½ teaspoon pure vanilla extract

1¼ cups unbleached all-purpose flour

1½ teaspoons baking powder

¼ teaspoon salt

½ cup whole milk, at room temperature

Vanilla or *dulce de leche* ice cream, optional

. . . .

spoon or spatula, draping over the fruit in long bands (don't try to spread it or it will sink into the fruit). Gently blend the bands of batter together until it covers the fruit in a single layer.

4   Place a baking sheet or a piece of foil under the cobbler to catch any juices that may bubble over. Bake for 50 to 60 minutes, until the topping is nicely browned and a toothpick or skewer inserted into the topping comes out clean. Serve warm, accompanied by vanilla or *dulce de leche* ice cream.

Classic
Strawberry Shortcakes

MAKES 8 SHORTCAKES

These big, pillowy shortcakes are tender and slightly sweet. Split in half and filled with juicy strawberries, they are topped with softly whipped cream for a gorgeous dessert. Ripe, flavorful strawberries are essential for this dessert, as is sugaring them beforehand to let the natural juices come out.

1   Cut the cold butter into small cubes and refrigerate for 10 minutes. Put the milk in a cup, add 1 tablespoon of vanilla to it, and refrigerate it as well. Line a baking sheet with parchment paper.

2   Put the flour, ¼ cup sugar, baking powder, and salt in a large bowl and whisk until blended. Scatter the cold butter pieces over the dry ingredients and toss them with your hands until they are coated. With a pastry blender, cut the butter into smaller and smaller pieces. If chunks of cold butter get stuck in the wires of the pastry blender, use a table knife to push them off, then continue cutting. You are done when the biggest butter pieces are not larger than green peas. Some will be much smaller, and that's fine.

3   Pour the chilled vanilla milk into the flour and butter, then stir with the fork 12 to 15 times, until it holds together in big, shaggy clumps. Sprinkle your work surface with a little flour.

Ingredients

½ cup (1 stick) cold unsalted butter

¾ cup milk

1 tablespoon plus 1 teaspoon pure vanilla extract

2 cups unbleached all-purpose flour

¼ cup plus 5 tablespoons sugar

2½ teaspoons baking powder

¼ teaspoon salt

6 cups (2½ pounds) fresh ripe strawberries

1½ cups heavy whipping cream

Turn the clumpy mass out onto the floury surface and knead it gently 4 to 8 times, until it comes together into a dough. Don't knead too long or the shortbread will be tough.

4   Pat the dough into an 8 by 4-inch rectangle. Be sure it is the same thickness everywhere. Cut the rectangle in half lengthwise, and then into quarters crosswise. You should have 8 pieces, each about 2 inches square. Brush off any extra flour from the top and bottom of the shortcakes and place them several inches apart on the prepared baking sheet. Refrigerate for 20 minutes. Just after you slip the shortcakes into the refrigerator, position an oven rack in the center of the oven and preheat the oven to 425°F.

5   Bake for 14 to 16 minutes, until golden brown on top and firm to the touch. Transfer the pan to a cooling rack. Let the shortcakes cool completely.

6   Place the berries in a sieve or colander under cool running water. Look through them and discard any moldy berries. Drain well and pat dry with paper towels. Remove the leafy green tops from the strawberries. Cut the strawberries into ¼-inch-thick slices. Put the berries in a medium bowl, sprinkle with 3 tablespoons of sugar, and toss. Stir every few minutes. As the berries sit, the sugar will draw out some of their juices and make a tasty syrup in the bottom of the bowl.

7   Put the cream, the remaining 2 tablespoons sugar, and the remaining 1 teaspoon vanilla in a medium bowl. Whip the cream until it holds medium-firm peaks when the whisk or beaters are lifted. It should look silky. If you whip the cream too long and it looks grainy, lumpy, or curdled, pour in 3 or 4 more tablespoons cream and stir in gently (no more whipping). It should smooth out nicely. Cover until needed.

8   Cut each shortcake in half. Put one of the bottoms, cut side up, on each plate. Spoon the strawberries and syrup over the bottoms, dividing evenly. Place a large spoonful of whipped cream on top of each mound of strawberries. Set the biscuit tops, cut sides down, on the cream. Serve right away.

Chocolate Chip Cookies

MAKES ABOUT 60 COOKIES

Few among us can resist the mouthwatering aroma of butter, brown sugar, and chocolate that reminds of all things warm and wonderful. While many versions of this American classic exist, this is a favorite, bursting with chunks of both semisweet and milk chocolate, with an extra splash of vanilla for a deep, round flavor.

1 Preheat the oven to 350°F and position an oven rack in the center. Line two baking sheets with parchment paper.

2 Place the butter, granulated sugar, and brown sugar in the bowl of a stand mixer and beat on medium-low speed until smooth and blended, about 2 minutes. Or use a hand mixer and a medium bowl, although you may need to beat the batter a little longer to achieve the same results. Scrape down the bowl. Add the eggs, one at a time, and beat just until blended after each addition. Add the vanilla and blend well. Scrape down the bowl.

3 Whisk together the flour, baking soda, and salt in a medium bowl. Turn the mixer to the lowest speed and add the dry ingredients all at once. Blend just until there are no more patches of flour. Scrape down the bowl.

4 Add the chocolate chunks and the nuts, if using, and blend on low speed just until combined. Remove the bowl from the mixer and stir gently a few times to make sure there are no more patches of unincorporated flour or butter lurking near the bottom.

5 Using a small ice-cream scoop or spoon, portion tablespoon-sized mounds onto the prepared baking sheets, spacing them about 2 inches apart. Bake the cookies one sheet at a time, rotating the sheet halfway through, for 10 to 14 minutes, until the cookies are golden brown at the edges and still a bit pale in the center. If you want crisp cookies instead of chewy ones, bake for a couple of extra minutes. Transfer the cookies to a cooling rack and let them cool completely before serving.

Chewy Oatmeal Cookies

MAKES 42 COOKIES

There's nothing better than a chewy oatmeal cookie, crisp around the edges and soft in the center. These nubby snacks come with a hint of cinnamon and a few bumps of tangy red cranberries to add contrast and color.

1 Position one oven rack in the top third of the oven and one oven rack in the bottom third of the oven, and preheat the oven to 350°F. Line two baking sheets with parchment paper.

2 Put the butter and both sugars in a large bowl. Using a mixer, beat on low speed for 1 minute. Turn up the speed to medium and beat for another minute. The mixture should be blended and smooth. Scrape down the sides of the bowl. Add the egg and vanilla and beat on medium-low speed until well blended. Scrape down the sides of the bowl.

3 Put the flour, baking soda, salt, and cinnamon in a medium bowl and whisk until blended. Add the dry ingredients to the liquid in the mixer bowl and beat on low speed just until only a few patches of flour remain. Add the rolled oats and cranberries and continue to beat on low speed until no patches of flour are visible and the ingredients are evenly blended. Scrape down the bowl and make sure there are no clumps of flour hiding in the bottom of the bowl.

4 Use an ice-cream scoop to shape the dough into cookies, or shape the dough by measuring out 1 level tablespoon for each cookie and then rolling the dough between your palms into a ball. Space the balls about 1½ inches apart on the prepared baking sheets.

5 Place one baking sheet on each oven rack. Bake for 7 minutes, then switch the pans between the oven racks. Bake for another 6 to 7 minutes, until the cookies are golden brown around the edges. Transfer the pan to cooling racks and let the cookies cool completely. You may need to reuse the pans to finish baking all the cookies. Let the pans cool before you put more dough on them for baking. Store in an airtight container or a resealable plastic bag for up to 1 week.

Classic

Fudgy Brownies

MAKES 16 (2-INCH) BROWNIES

Rich, dark, fudgy, and slightly chewy, these homemade brownies are always a hit, so much better than anything you can buy. Serve cold with a glass of milk, or warm from the oven with a scoop of ice cream. Like a simple black dress, they can be accessorized to match any occasion. For a casual snack, serve them right out of the pan. For something a bit dressier, dust the brownies with a layer of powdered sugar. Or drizzle melted dark chocolate (or dark, milk, and/or white chocolate) wildly over the top.

1 Preheat the oven to 350°F and position an oven rack in the center. Line an 8-inch square cake pan with foil or parchment paper across the bottom and up two of the sides, then lightly coat with an oil spray.

2 Bring 2 inches of water to a boil in the bottom of a double boiler. Place the butter, semisweet chocolate, and unsweetened chocolate in the top of the double boiler (off the heat). Turn off the heat, then set the butter and chocolate over the steaming water. Stir occasionally until the chocolate is melted and smooth.

3 Remove from the heat and whisk in the sugar. Whisk in the eggs, one at a time, stirring well to incorporate each before adding the next. Stir in the vanilla. Whisk in the flour and salt. Continue to stir until the batter changes from dull and

broken-looking to smooth and shiny, about 1 minute. Whisk in the chocolate chips and chopped nuts, if using.

4   Scrape the batter into the prepared pan and spread evenly. Bake for 35 to 40 minutes, until a skewer inserted into the center of the brownies comes out with a few moist crumbs clinging to it (do not overbake). Transfer to a rack and cool completely.

5   Run a thin knife or flexible spatula around the edges of the pan to loosen the brownies. Grasp the foil or parchment paper extending up the sides and pull gently upward. Set the brownies on a cutting surface and cut into 16 equal pieces. Since these are fudgy, keep a hot, wrung-out wet towel nearby so you can wipe the knife clean between slices. You could also serve the brownies right out of the pan if you like, pressing a piece of plastic wrap against any cut surfaces and across the top to keep them fresh. Tightly wrap the remaining brownies in plastic or place in an airtight container. They will keep well at room temperature for 2 to 3 days or in the refrigerator for up to 5 days.

Chocolate Pudding

Ingredients

7 ounces good-quality milk chocolate, finely chopped

1¼ cups plus 5 tablespoons heavy whipping cream

1¼ cups whole milk

¼ cup sugar

1 large egg

4 large egg yolks

1½ ounces semisweet or bittersweet chocolate, chopped

Softly whipped cream, for serving

Milk or dark chocolate curls, for serving (optional)

SERVES 6

Milk chocolate is often overlooked in the quest for the newest and darkest desserts, but it's still a favorite with kids and adults alike. Its presence is a surprise in this recipe, as the luscious milk chocolate custard is hidden under a thin layer of warm, dark chocolate ganache. So although the spoon dips into a dark surface, it comes out with the lighter custard full of the malty, caramel-like qualities of milk chocolate. The interplay of cool, milky sweetness against warm, dark richness is sublime.

1   Preheat the oven to 325°F and position an oven rack in the center.

2   Place the chocolate in a medium bowl. Heat the milk, 1¼ cups cream, milk, and sugar in a medium saucepan over medium heat until just before it boils. Immediately pour it over the chopped chocolate. Let it sit for 1 minute, then whisk gently but thoroughly to blend completely. Combine the egg and egg yolks in a small bowl. Add to the chocolate, whisking to incorporate thoroughly.

3   Pour the chocolate custard through a strainer into a pitcher or large measuring cup with spout. Place six 6-ounce ramekins or custard cups in a large roasting pan, making sure they don't touch, and divide the warm custard among them. Pull out the oven rack and place the pan on the rack; then remove one of the cups, pour enough hot (not boiling) tap water into that area

to come halfway up the sides of the cups, and replace the cup. Cut a piece of foil large enough to fit just inside the edges of the pan, then lay the foil across the top of the cups, making sure it doesn't touch the custard. You may need to smooth and flatten the foil on the counter if any wrinkles touch the custard. Gently push the rack back into the oven, shut the oven door, and bake the custards for 50 to 60 minutes, just until the edges of the custards are set—there should be a dime-sized liquid area in the very center of the custard (test by gently tapping the side of the pan).

4   Remove the foil and then the pan from the oven, being careful not to tilt the pan and splash water on top of the custards. Set the pan on a heatproof surface. Use tongs (or your hand protected by a kitchen towel) to immediately remove the cups from the water bath and place them on a rack to cool to room temperature, about 40 minutes. Cover with plastic wrap and refrigerate until cold, at least 4 hours or overnight.

5   Place the semisweet chocolate in a small bowl. Heat the remaining 5 tablespoons cream in a small saucepan over medium heat just until it begins to simmer (do not allow the cream to boil and evaporate). Immediately pour the cream over the chocolate. Allow it to sit undisturbed for 1 minute, then gently stir until thoroughly blended and smooth to create a ganache. Spoon a tablespoon of the ganache onto the surface of each custard, then gently swirl each cup until the dark chocolate completely covers the custard. (If the ganache seems too thick to spread easily, heat another tablespoon of cream and mix it in.)

6   Serve the custards immediately, while the ganache is still warm, or refrigerate for up to 1 hour. As the ganache chills, it hardens and pulls away from the sides or the cup, losing its silken texture or exposing the custard beneath, thereby spoiling the surprise. Serve each with a spoonful of whipped cream, topped with a scattering of chocolate curls if you like.

Old-Fashioned, Better-Than-Any-Box
Butterscotch Pudding

SERVES 6

Yes, it's more work to make this pudding from scratch than from a box, but the payoff is hugely delicious. This pudding is creamy when warm, thick and silky once it's chilled for a few hours—it's your choice how you enjoy it. A generous amount of salt balances the brown sugar sweetness, and for a touch of tang, you could top each pudding with a spoonful of crème fraîche. Plan ahead, as the pudding needs to cool for at least three hours.

1 Preheat the oven to 300°F. Melt the butter in a medium, heavy-based saucepan over medium-high heat. Add the brown sugar and stir with a wooden spoon or heatproof rubber spatula until blended. Bring the thick sugar mixture to a boil and cook, stirring and scraping, for about 4 minutes from the time it starts to bubble. At first it will look puffy and frothy, but eventually it turns smoother and creamier as the moisture cooks off. Scrape the sides and bottom of the pan well so the sugar caramelizes but doesn't burn.

2 Carefully pour in the cream and milk. It will sizzle and the sugar will seize up in a lump, but that's okay. Gently whisk the mixture over medium heat until all the sugar has melted and the mixture is smooth. Whisk in the salt and vanilla.

Ingredients

3 tablespoons unsalted butter
1 cup dark brown sugar
2 cups heavy cream
½ cup whole milk
1 teaspoon coarse salt
½ teaspoon pure vanilla extract
1 large egg
5 large egg yolks

3   Put the egg and yolks into a medium bowl
and whisk until blended. Gently whisk in the
hot cream until well blended, but don't whisk
vigorously because you don't want to work air
into the pudding.

4   Put six 6-ounce ramekins or pudding cups
into a 13 by 9-inch baking dish and pour the
pudding batter into the cups. Add very hot
water to the baking dish so it comes halfway
up the ramekins. Cover the whole dish with
foil and carefully transfer the dish to the oven.
Don't let the water slosh into the puddings.
Bake until the edges of the puddings are
set and the centers are still quite wobbly,
45 to 50 minutes. Remove the dish from
the oven, take the puddings from the water
bath using tongs or a kitchen towel to protect
your hands, and let them cool for about an
hour on a rack. Cover each with plastic and
transfer to the fridge to chill for at least 3
hours or up to 3 days.

Chocolate Chunk

Bread Pudding

SERVES 8

Bread pudding is one of the best ways to warm friends on a cool night. Golden brown on top, soft and custardy within, it's made by pouring a sweet, eggy cream over dried bread. Chocolate chunks add a welcome burst of flavor, and if the bread pudding is warm, they might be meltingly soft.

1 Position an oven rack in the center of the oven and preheat the oven to 325°F. Lightly butter or spray a 9 by 2-inch pie dish or round cake pan.

2 Cut the crust off the bread and throw the crust away. Then cut or tear the bread into ½-inch cubes or pieces. Spread the cubes on the baking sheet and bake for 20 minutes. This will dry out the bread so it can soak up the custard. Transfer the baking sheet to a cooling rack and let cool completely. Measure out 4 cups of bread cubes for the pudding. Transfer any remaining bread cubes to a resealable plastic bag and store in the cupboard (or freezer) for another use.

3 Whisk together the eggs, egg yolks, sugar, and salt in a medium bowl until completely blended. Whisk in the milk, cream, and vanilla and blend well. Add the toasted bread cubes and stir them into the custard. Cover with plastic wrap and refrigerate for 20 minutes, then stir to make sure the bread soaks up the

custard evenly. Return to the refrigerator for another 10 to 20 minutes, or until the bread has soaked up most of the custard and looks very soft.

4   Stir the chopped chocolate into the soaked bread. Make sure the chocolate is evenly distributed. Scrape into the prepared baking dish and press it into an even layer. Bake the bread pudding for 50 to 70 minutes, or until slightly puffed, golden brown, and set in the center. To check for doneness, press down firmly in the center of the bread pudding with a spoon. The pudding is done when the center feels firm. If the custard pools around the spoon, return it to the oven and bake for another 10 to 15 minutes, then check again. Transfer to a cooling rack and let cool for 15 to 20 minutes. Serve with whipped cream. Cover any leftovers and refrigerate for up to 4 days. Reheat in a 325°F oven for 20 to 25 minutes, or until warmed through.

Vanilla Cupcakes
with Chocolate Frosting

....
Ingredients

Frosting

**6 ounces semisweet chocolate,
chopped into small pieces**

¾ cup heavy whipping cream

Cupcake Batter

**1½ cups unbleached all-purpose
flour**

¾ teaspoon baking soda

¼ teaspoon salt

3 large eggs, at room temperature

1 tablespoon pure vanilla extract

**¾ cup (1½ sticks) unsalted butter,
softened**

¾ cup sugar

½ cup buttermilk

**Sprinkles, confetti candy, coarse
sugar, or any edible decorations**

....

MAKES 12 CUPCAKES

Something about cupcakes makes people (and kids!) smile, and these golden cupcakes with chocolate icing are no exception. Single-serving sizes of cake, they get their tenderness and tang from buttermilk. Pack cupcakes into lunch boxes, keep them for an after-school snack, or make a double recipe for an informal party or picnic.

1 Position an oven rack in the center of the oven and preheat the oven to 350°F. Line a standard 12-cup muffin pan with paper liners.

2 Make the frosting by putting the chocolate pieces into a medium bowl. Pour the cream into a small saucepan and place over medium heat, just until it begins to boil. Turn off the heat. Immediately pour the cream over the chocolate. Let it sit for 2 minutes, then whisk gently until blended and smooth. Set aside to cool, whisking gently every 15 to 20 minutes, until the chocolate has the consistency of a creamy frosting. You can even do this the night before, cover it with plastic wrap, and leave it on the counter.

3 Make the cupcake batter by sifting the flour, baking soda, and salt together into a medium bowl. Crack the eggs into a small bowl and add the vanilla. Beat the eggs lightly with a fork, just until evenly mixed.

4 Place the softened butter and sugar in a large bowl. Using a stand mixer, cream the butter and sugar for 6 to 7 minutes, until the mixture is very light, almost white, in color. Turn off the mixer. Scrape down the sides of the bowl. With the mixer running on medium speed, add the beaten eggs slowly, about a tablespoon at a time. Let each addition blend into the butter mixture completely (it will only take about 5 seconds) before adding the next. Scrape down the sides of the bowl. Add half the dry ingredients to the bowl. Turn the mixer on low speed and beat just until the dry ingredients are just blended, then repeat with the remaining flour and the buttermilk. Mix only until you don't see any more dry patches. Scrape down the bowl one last time, and make sure there aren't any dry bits of butter clumps hiding in the bottom of the bowl.

5 Divide the batter evenly among the prepared muffin cups. They should be no more than half full. Bake for 20 minutes, or until the tops of the cupcakes are firm to the touch and a toothpick inserted into the center comes out clean. Transfer the pan to a cooling rack and let the cupcakes cool completely (at least 40 minutes) before topping with frosting.

6 Place the cupcakes on a work surface or a piece of parchment paper. Divide the frosting evenly among the cupcake tops. There is enough frosting for about 2 level tablespoons on each cupcake. Spread the icing close to the edges. Decorate the top with sprinkles or whatever you like. Keep the cupcakes at room temperature for 2 days, and then store any leftovers in the refrigerator.

Extraordinary
Ice Cream Sundaes Three Ways

SERVES 6

Back in the days of the soda fountain, a sundae made with chocolate sauce, whipped cream, and a cherry on top was enough to thrill, but nowadays our sophisticated palates want something a notch more exciting than that. Here are three combos that are both simple and sophisticated. Make the sundaes as suggested here or mix and match to create your own. If you have leftover sauces, they will keep covered in the fridge for a week or so.

1   Put the granulated sugar, corn syrup, and water into a small, heavy saucepan. Bring to a boil over medium-high heat, stirring just until the sugar has dissolved. Boil for 6 to 7 minutes, until the sauce is a deep amber, fragrant with caramel, and you see just a few wisps of smoke. Be careful because the caramel is extremely hot. Take the pan off the heat and add the cream. It will bubble like crazy. Whisk until the sauce is blended and smooth, then whisk in the 2 teaspoons butter, vanilla, and salt. It will thicken a bit as it cools; keep slightly warm.

2   Heat the oven to 425°F. Cut the pineapple in half lengthwise, cut away the core, and then cut each piece lengthwise again to make long strips. Cut away the skin, and lay the pineapple

strips on a rimmed baking sheet. Brush with the melted butter and sprinkle on the brown sugar. Roast for about 10 minutes, then turn the strips and continue roasting until the pineapple is soft and starting to brown and sizzle around the edges. Let cool, then chop coarsely and transfer to a bowl, scraping up the juices as long as they're not burnt. Keep warm.

3   Put a scoop of ice cream in each of six bowls. Spoon over some pineapple, then add another scoop of ice cream and more pineapple. Squirt on a little cloud of whipped cream, drizzle the sundae with caramel sauce, and sprinkle with the macadamias. Serve immediately.

• •

With Dark Chocolate Mint Sauce and Crushed Peppermint Candy

4 ounces dark chocolate (up to 70% cacao), chopped
¾ cup heavy whipping cream
¼ teaspoon peppermint extract
6 peppermint hard candies or mini candy canes
1 quart vanilla ice cream
Whipped cream (from a can is fine, as long as it's real cream)

• •

1   Put the chopped chocolate in a medium bowl. Put the cream in a small saucepan and bring just to a simmer. Pour the cream over the chocolate, let sit for 1 minute, then gently whisk until the sauce is smooth and homogenous. Stir in the peppermint extract. Keep slightly warm.

2   Crush the candies into small bits by putting them in a heavy plastic bag and smashing with a hammer, meat mallet, or the edge of a heavy pot.

3   Put a scoop of ice cream in each of six bowls. Sprinkle over some crushed peppermint candies, then add another scoop of ice cream and more candies. Squirt on a little cloud of whipped cream, and drizzle the sundae with the chocolate-mint sauce. Serve immediately.

••••••••••••••••••••••••••••

With Roasted Strawberries with Brown Sugar–Balsamic Drizzle

1 pound fresh strawberries, hulled and halved if very large

½ cup granulated sugar

¾ cup balsamic vinegar

¼ cup dark brown sugar

¼ teaspoon pure vanilla extract

Tiny pinch of salt

1 quart vanilla ice cream

Whipped cream (from a can is fine, as long as it's real cream)

⅓ cup toasted sliced almonds

••••••••••••••••••••••••••••

1 Preheat the oven to 400°F. Toss the strawberries and granulated sugar together, then spread onto a rimmed baking sheet. Roast until the berries are softened and the juices are running, 15 to 20 minutes. Scrape into a bowl and chill.

2 Put the vinegar and brown sugar in a small pot and bring to a simmer, stirring to dissolve the sugar. Simmer until reduced and nicely syrupy (it will thicken more as it cools), about 12 minutes. Add the vanilla and salt. Cool slightly.

3 Put a scoop of ice cream in each of six bowls. Spoon over some strawberries, then add another scoop of ice cream and more berries. Squirt on a little cloud of whipped cream, drizzle the sundae with the balsamic glaze, and sprinkle with the almonds. Serve immediately.

Acknowledgments

Make this book special—warm, inviting, comforting old favorites with new spins that conjure up those same feelings you had while eating comfort food as a child. That was the gauntlet that was thrown down and then taken up by Martha Holmberg, the creative department of Sur La Table, JohnsonRauhoff, and Andrews McMeel Publishing.

Thanks to Martha for creating time-honored favorites with a contemporary spin. For bringing those favorites to life on the pages of *Simple Comforts: 50 Heartwarming Recipes*, thanks go to the creative department of Sur La Table led by Robb Ginter with the support of Bryan Habeck, Felicia Chao, Dean Fuller, Rebecca Burgess, and the JohnsonRauhoff studio.

Thanks also to Marie Simmons, Cindy Mushet, Sara Jay, and Rick Rodgers for their recipe contributions. Andrews McMeel met the challenge due to the great work of Holly Ogden, Ren-Wei Harn, John Carroll, and Carol Coe, with the support of Kirsty Melville and Jean Lucas. And finally, thanks to Kathy Tierney for her continued inspiration in creating great books that speak to our customers.

Metric Conversions and Equivalents

Metric Conversion Formulas

TO CONVERT	MULTIPLY
Ounces to grams	Ounces by 28.35
Pounds to kilograms	Pounds by .454
Teaspoons to milliliters	Teaspoons by 4.93
Tablespoons to milliliters	Tablespoons by 14.79
Fluid ounces to milliliters	Fluid ounces by 29.57
Cups to milliliters	Cups by 236.59
Cups to liters	Cups by .236
Pints to liters	Pints by .473
Quarts to liters	Quarts by .946
Gallons to liters	Gallons by 3.785
Inches to centimeters	Inches by 2.54

Approximate Metric Equivalents

VOLUME

¼ teaspoon	1 milliliter
½ teaspoon	2.5 milliliters
¾ teaspoon	4 milliliters
1 teaspoon	5 milliliters
2 teaspoons	10 milliliters
1 tablespoon (½ fluid ounce)	15 milliliters
¼ cup	60 milliliters
⅓ cup	80 milliliters
½ cup (4 fluid ounces)	120 milliliters
⅔ cup	160 milliliters
¾ cup	180 milliliters
1 cup (8 fluid ounces)	240 milliliters
2 cups (1 pint)	460 milliliters
3 cups	700 milliliters
4 cups (1 quart)	.95 liter
1 quart plus ¼ cup	1 liter
4 quarts (1 gallon)	3.8 liters

WEIGHT

¼ ounce	7 grams
½ ounce	14 grams
¾ ounce	21 grams
1 ounce	28 grams
2 ounces	57 grams
3 ounces	85 grams
4 ounces (¼ pound)	113 grams
5 ounces	142 grams
6 ounces	170 grams
7 ounces	198 grams
8 ounces (½ pound)	227 grams
16 ounces (1 pound)	454 grams
35.25 ounces (2.2 pounds)	1 kilogram

LENGTH

¼ inch	6 millimeters
½ inch	1¼ centimeters
1 inch	2½ centimeters
2 inches	5 centimeters
6 inches	15¼ centimeters
12 inches (1 foot)	30 centimeters

Oven Temperatures
To convert Fahrenheit to Celsius, subtract 32 from Fahrenheit, multiply the result by 5, then divide by 9.

Description	Fahrenheit	Celsius	British Gas Mark
Very cool	200°	95°	0
Very cool	225°	110°	¼
Very cool	250°	120°	½
Cool	275°	135°	1
Cool	300°	150°	2
Warm	325°	165°	3
Moderate	350°	175°	4
Moderately hot	375°	190°	5
Fairly hot	400°	200°	6
Hot	425°	220°	7
Very hot	450°	230°	8
Very hot	475°	245°	9

Common Ingredients and Their Approximate Equivalents
1 cup uncooked rice = 225 grams
1 cup all-purpose flour = 140 grams
1 stick butter (4 ounces • ½ cup • 8 tablespoons) = 110 grams
1 cup butter (8 ounces • 2 sticks • 16 tablespoons) = 220 grams
1 cup brown sugar, firmly packed = 225 grams
1 cup granulated sugar = 200 grams

Information compiled from *Recipes into Type* by Joan Whitman and Dolores Simon (Newton, MA: Biscuit Books, 2000); *The New Food Lover's Companion* by Sharon Tyler Herbst (Hauppauge, NY: Barron's, 1995); and *Rosemary Brown's Big Kitchen Instruction Book* (Kansas City, MO: Andrews McMeel, 1998).

Index